THE POETRY OF OUR LORD

THE POETRY OF OUR LORD

An Examination of the Formal Elements of Hebrew Poetry in the Discourses of Jesus Christ

BY THE

REV. C. F. BURNEY, M.A., D.Litt.
Oriel Professor of the Interpretation of Holy Scripture at Oxford
Hon. D.D. Durham; Fellow of Oriel and St. John's Colleges, Oxford; Canon of Rochester

WIPF & STOCK · Eugene, Oregon

Wipf and Stock Publishers
199 W 8th Ave, Suite 3
Eugene, OR 97401

The Poetry of Our Lord
An Examination of the Formal Elements of Hebrew Poetry
in the Discourses of Jesus Christ
By Burney, C. F.
ISBN 13: 978-1-60608-295-9
Publication date 11/24/2008
Previously published by Clarendon Press, 1925

Yihyū́ lᵉrāṣṓn ’imrē-phī́
wᵉhegyṓn libbī́
Lᵉphānḗkā Yahwḗh tāmī́d
ṣūrī́ wᵉgō’ᵃlī́

"Let the wórds of my moúth be accéptable,
and the meditátion of my heárt,
Before Theé, O Lórd, contínually,
my Róck and my Redeémer."

PREFACE

THE scheme of this work first began to take shape in the author's mind while he was collecting material for his *Aramaic Origin of the Fourth Gospel.* Close examination of the language of this Gospel brought home to him its frequent resemblance in style to the diction of the Old Testament writers—Prophets, Psalmists, and Wise men, whose utterances are cast in poetic form, the chief characteristic of which is adherence to certain rules of composition which are defined by the terms Parallelism and Rhythm. In studying the Fourth Gospel in its formal aspect, the first fact which strikes the eye is our Lord's free use of Parallelism, and that especially of the kind which is known as Antithetic. Observation of this characteristic at once invites comparison with the form of His teaching as recorded by the Synoptists; and the result which emerges is that this Hebraic style of expression is equally well marked in the sources employed by these latter. Examples of Antithetic Parallelism were therefore collected by the writer among his other statistics for his book on the Fourth Gospel, on the ground that they would serve both to prove the Palestinian origin of the discourses contained in the Gospel, and also to illustrate their connexion with the Synoptic discourses, thus advancing an argument which undoubtedly favours their substantial authenticity. On further consideration, however, it appeared that this line of research was not strictly germane to the argument for the Aramaic origin of the Gospel, but rather demanded a separate study which might illustrate the formal connexion of much of our Lord's teaching with the Hebrew poetry of the Old Testament, and also serve as a guide in determining whether we can rely that we possess in the Gospels something approaching to, if not actually representing, the *ipsissima verba* of His teaching.

To speak of hoping to ascertain the actual words of Christ may seem bold, if not foolish; but is it really a vain hope? Take, for example, the Lord's Prayer, in which the existence of a well-marked rhythm (p. 112) and rhyme (p. 113) can hardly be gainsaid. It is obvious that these traits must have been intended by our Lord as an aid to memory, and would have acted as such; hence it is scarcely overbold to believe that the Matthaean tradition represents the actual words of the prayer as they issued from His lips. So with other sayings which exhibit the formal characteristics of Hebrew poetry. Conformity to a certain type which can be abundantly exemplified—and that not only in one source, but in all the sources which go to form the Gospels—is surely a strong argument for substantial authenticity. For the alternative is that the different authors of the sources, if they possessed merely a vague recollection or tradition of the sayings, must have set themselves, one and all, to dress them in a parallelistic and rhythmical form; and that various writers, and in fact all writers to whom we owe records of our Lord's teaching, should have essayed independently to do the same thing, and so doing should have produced results which are essentially identical in form, is surely out of the question.

There are, of course, marked variations in the recorded wording of Christ's teaching; and, even when we have made allowance for the probability that on different occasions He may have conveyed the same teaching in a somewhat varying form, it is clear that the greater part of such instances witnesses to a certain freedom in the recording of His utterances. Of two varying records one at least departs to some extent from the original in wording if not in sense. This is most marked in the two forms in which the great Discourse-document, commonly known as Q, has come down to us in the First and Third Gospels. The present writer confidently hopes that the criterion of poetical form which he puts forward may be of service in determining which version of Q has the better claim to be considered a literally faithful record. If his deductions are correct, it appears that in most cases, though not in all, the verdict should go to the First Gospel. St. Matthew—if he may be considered as the author of Q—was a faithful recorder of Christ's teaching in its original Semitic style; and the editor who embodied his work in the First Gospel was very like the Hebrew redactors of the historical books of the Old Testament, content to reproduce the *ipsissima verba* of his source, even though he does not hesitate to gloss them here and there by his own additions. St. Luke, on the other hand, was more closely akin to a modern historian in his method. For him the substance, rather than the form, of the teaching appears to have been the all-important consideration; and, while he was clearly a skilful and faithful recorder of the substance, he certainly seems to have held himself free to alter the form in cases in which Synonymous Parallelism might appear redundant to Gentile readers, and to clothe his record in a graceful Greek dress which not infrequently involved paraphrase and changes in the order of words.

Another subject of inquiry on which the writer believes that his method of examination sheds some light is the question whether St. Mark knew and used Q. Evidence adduced in the present volume should go far to prove that this was the case. Such a conclusion emerges first through comparison of certain antithetically parallel sayings of our Lord as given by Mark and by the other Gospels, from which it appears that a characteristic clear-cut form of antithesis, preserved by these latter and attested by numerous parallels, has been to some extent lost in Mark through the addition of new matter (cf. p. 74). The inference is that the other Synoptists cannot, in these passages, have been drawing from Mark, but that both they and Mark were dependent upon a common source (Q), to which they have adhered more faithfully than he. This might, it is true, be parried by the possibility that St. Mark's Gospel may have received some amount of accretion in the form of glosses after it left his hands; but against this explanation stands the fact that the passages in question do not offer the only evidence which seems to indicate Mark's use of Q. While referring to the foot-notes on pp. 74, 75, the writer would point in particular to his separation (p. 118) of the passage Mark 13^{9-13} out of Mark's 'little apocalypse' solely on the ground of its rhythmical form, before he was aware of the fact that precisely this passage stands in Matt. 10^{17-22} in a wholly different context; and to his rejection of Mark 13^{10} ('And to all nations first must the gospel be preached') in this passage as a gloss, on rhythmical grounds, before noticing that the verse was actually absent from the parallel passage Luke 21^{12-19}, and from Matt. 10^{17-22}. The natural inference, based on the rhythmical distinction of Mark 13^{9-13} from its context, and upon the fact that the passage occurs in a different context in Matthew, is that it is a discourse, not eschatological in original intent, which Mark has borrowed from Q and set in the midst of an eschatological discourse; and which Matthew has likewise embodied from Q and placed (or retained) in a more appropriate position, viz. in connexion with other discourses bearing on the commission of the disciples. Matthew has also adopted the same passage from Mark in *ch.* 24^{9-14}, i. e. the chapter which gives his version of the 'little apocalypse'; and here we see how the process of giving an eschatological character and setting to the passage, begun by Mark, has been carried still further.

These are lines of research which emerge from the subject of this book. The writer does not profess to have worked them thoroughly, or, indeed, to have done more than to endeavour to solve such points as forced themselves upon his notice in studying our Lord's use of parallelism and rhythm. He hopes, however, that he may have attempted enough to convince other scholars that his method opens up a not altogether unfruitful field of investigation.

The Aramaic renderings of our Lord's sayings which form a marked feature in the book aim at conforming, so far as may be, with the Galilaean dialect, which was doubtless that spoken by our Lord and His disciples. For this the evidence can only be derived from sources dating from a period somewhat later than our Lord's day—the Aramaic sections of the Palestinian Talmud and the Midrashim, dating from the fourth to the sixth centuries A.D., and the Palestinian-Syriac Lectionary of unknown date. Though it is unfortunate that we do not possess any contemporary evidence for the Galilaean Aramaic of the first century A.D., it is unlikely that the dialect underwent any substantial change during the four or five centuries following; and the evidence which we possess in the sources above mentioned may be taken as fairly reliable. The writer feels bound to acknowledge his deep debt to Dr. Gustaf Dalman's *Grammatik des jüdisch-palästinischen Aramäisch* (2e Aufl. 1905), which offers a detailed and profoundly learned study of Jewish Aramaic, and, in particular, is wonderfully helpful upon the side of the Galilaean idiom and vocabulary. Without this invaluable guide it would have been impossible to have undertaken the present study. Within the past few months a small but most useful *Grammar of Palestinian Jewish Aramaic* has been produced by Prof. W. B. Stevenson, of Glasgow, and this should prove very valuable to English students of the language who need an introduction to Dalman's much larger work, or who have not a knowledge of German sufficient for the utilization of the latter.

The writer is well aware that he has been very bold in attempting an Aramaic rendering of so considerable a portion of our Lord's sayings, and freely acknowledges that he is likely to have been guilty of a considerable number of errors. The detection of these may form an exercise for the learning and ingenuity of scholars who, though they perhaps would not themselves have ventured on the perilous task which he has undertaken, may with justice hold themselves competent to criticize the result when it is set before them. All such criticisms he will welcome as a contribution to the advancement of the study, only asking that conviction of errors in rendering may be set merely against his own competence, and not against the validity of the method which he has attempted to follow.

In quotation of our Lord's sayings square brackets [ ] are used to suggest that the words within them may be later accretions to the actual words of the Speaker, and (very rarely[1]) angular brackets ⟨ ⟩ to suggest that certain words may have been accidentally omitted from the records.

C. F. B.

OXFORD, *December*, 1924.

[1] Three times only—Matt. 5^{15}, Matt. 11^{26} = Luke 10^{21} b, Matt. 25^{39}.

[*The Author died on 15 April, 1925.*]

CONTENTS

PAGE

I. THE FORMAL CHARACTERISTICS OF HEBREW POETRY:—

Parallelism 15
Synonymous 16
Antithetic 20
Synthetic or Constructive 21
Rhythm 22
Four-beat 22
Three-beat 29
Ḳīnā 34
The Principles of Stress-accentuation in Hebrew Poetry 43
Appended note on the theory of Rabbi Azariah 59

II. THE USE OF PARALLELISM BY OUR LORD:—

Synonymous Parallelism 63
Antithetic Parallelism 71
Synthetic Parallelism 89
Step-Parallelism 90
A further point of connexion between the Fourth Gospel and the Synoptists . . 96

III. THE USE OF RHYTHM BY OUR LORD:—

Preliminary remarks 100
Four-beat Rhythm 112
Three-beat Rhythm 130
Ḳīnā-Rhythm 137

PAGE

IV. THE USE OF RHYME BY OUR LORD:—

Rhyme almost unused in most of the literary poetry of the Old Testament 147
Its use in the Folk-poetry of the Hebrews . 148
Its use in the Gnomic literature of the Hebrews 154
Enhanced facilities for Rhyme offered by Aramaic 160
Illustrations of the use of Rhyme by our Lord 161

INDEX OF BIBLICAL REFERENCES . . . 177

I

THE FORMAL CHARACTERISTICS OF HEBREW POETRY

Since the object of this discussion is to illustrate the fact that considerable portions of our Lord's recorded sayings and discourses are cast in the characteristic forms of Hebrew poetry, it is necessary at the outset briefly to indicate what these characteristics are, and to illustrate them from the poetry of the Old Testament. It should be observed that we are not primarily concerned with poetical thought and diction (which might characterize high-flown prose hardly less than poetry strictly so named), but with the *formal* characteristics of Hebrew poetry, which, when we meet them in the Old Testament writings, suffice to convince us that the writers are consciously employing poetry and not prose as the medium of their expression. These formal characteristics may be defined as two, viz. *Parallelism* and *Rhythm*.

Parallelism.

The use of the term *Parallelism*, and the apprehension of the importance of the phenomenon denoted by the term as a salient characteristic of Hebrew poetry, go back to a great Oxford scholar, Bishop Lowth, whose discussion in the introduction to his *Isaiah: A New Translation*, published in 1778, is the classical treatise on the subject.[1] Lowth distinguished three forms of Parallelism, which he termed respectively *Synonymous*, *Antithetic*, and *Synthetic* or *Constructive*. Among the important results established by him in his discussion, not the least was the fact that Parallelism is characteristic of the Prophetical writings no less than of the Hebrew books which are ordinarily reckoned as poetical, and that the former therefore properly fall into the same category as the latter.

§ *Synonymous Parallelism.*

This is a correspondence in idea between the two lines of a couplet, the second line reinforcing and as it were echoing the sense of the first in equivalent, though different, terms. As good an illustration of this as could be quoted from the Psalms is Ps. 114, in which this form of parallelism is clearly observable throughout.

1. 'When Israel came out of Egypt,
   The house of Jacob from among a strange people,
2. Judah became His sanctuary,
   Israel His dominion.
3. The sea beheld and fled,
   The Jordan turned backward.
4. The mountains skipped like rams,
   The hills like the young of the flock.
5. What aileth thee, O thou sea, that thou fleest?
   Thou Jordan, that thou turnest backward?
6. Ye mountains, that ye skip like rams?
   Ye hills, like the young of the flock?

[1] Cf. also the same scholar's dissertations on the subject, *De Sacra Poesi Hebraeorum, Praelectiones* xviii, xix.

7. Tremble, thou earth, at the presence of the Lord,
At the presence of the God of Jacob;
8. Who turneth the rock into a pool of water,
The flint into a springing well.'

The most perfect exemplification of this form of composition is when each member of the one line (e.g. subject, verb, and object) is reproduced by a corresponding term in the parallel line. So in Ps. $19^{1, 2}$:

'The heavens are telling the glory of God,
And the firmament declareth His handy-work.

Day unto day uttereth speech,
And night unto night sheweth knowledge.'

Ps. 94^{9}:

'He that planted the ear, shall He not hear?
Or He that formed the eye, shall He not see?'

Ps. 94^{16}:

'Who will rise up for me against evil-doers;
Who will take his stand for me against workers of wickedness?'

Ps. 101^{7}:

'Whoso worketh deceit shall not dwell in my house;
Whoso telleth lies shall not tarry in my sight.'

Such complete correspondence between each term of the parallel lines is not, of course, regularly carried out. Some one member of the first line (e.g. the verb, as in *vv.* $^{1, 2, 4, 6, 7, 8}$ of Ps. 114 above quoted) may extend its influence into the second line, and not be repeated by a synonym. Yet the general effect is the same and unmistakable, viz. the re-echoing of the thought of the first line in the second line of the couplet, producing (as Dr. Driver says) 'an effect which is at once grateful to the ear and satisfying to the mind'.[1]

Synonymous parallelism is highly characteristic of the oracles of Balaam. Thus the first oracle, Num. 23^{7-10}, runs as follows:

7. 'From Aram doth Balak bring me,
The king of Moab from the mountains of the east;

Come, curse thou me Jacob,
And come, denounce Israel.

8. How can I curse whom God hath not cursed?
And how can I denounce whom Yahweh hath not denounced?

9. For from the top of the rocks I see him,
And from the hills I espy him;

Lo, a people dwelling alone,
And not reckoning itself among the nations.

10. Who hath numbered the dust of Jacob?
And who hath counted the myriads of Israel?[2]

Let my soul die the death of the upright,
And be my last end like his.'

As examples of the use of this form of parallelism by the writing prophets we may notice the following passages:

Amos 5^{21-24}:

21. 'I hate, I despise your festivals,
And I delight not in your solemn assemblies.

22. Though ye offer Me burnt-offerings
And your meal-offerings, I will not accept them,

[1] *Introd. to the Literature of the O.T.*[9], p. 363.

[2] Reading וּמִי סָפַר אֶת־רִבְבֹת יִשְׂרָאֵל in place of וּמִסְפָּר אֶת־רֹבַע יִשְׂרָאֵל.

And the peace-offerings of your fatlings I will not regard.
23. Take away from Me the noise of thy songs,
And the melody of thy viols I will not hear:
24. But let justice roll down like water,
And righteousness like a perennial stream.'

Isa. 40^{29-31}:
29. 'He giveth power to the faint;
And to him that hath no might He increaseth strength.
30. Even youths may faint and grow weary,
And young warriors may utterly stumble;
31. But they that wait upon Yahweh shall renew their strength;
They shall put forth pinions like the eagles;
They shall run and not be weary;
They shall walk and not faint.'

Isa. $55^{6, 7}$:
6. 'Seek ye Yahweh while He may be found;
Call ye upon Him while He is near:
7. Let the wicked forsake his way,
And the unrighteous man his thoughts,
And let him return unto Yahweh, that He may have mercy upon him,
And unto our God, for He will abundantly pardon.'

In citing these illustrations, intentional selection has been made of passages in which synonymous parallelism is maintained through a number of consecutive verses. Very frequently, however, we find this form of parallelism employed in combination with the other forms which we have still to notice; and such combination of the different forms we shall see to be generally characteristic of our Lord's usage of parallelism.

§ *Antithetic Parallelism.*

Here the parallelism is carried out by *contrast* of the terms of the second line with those of the first. We may notice Ps. 1^6:

'For Yahweh knoweth the way of the righteous,
But the way of the ungodly shall perish.'

Ps. 10^{16}:

'Yahweh is king for ever and ever;
The heathen are perished out of His land.'

Ps. 11^5:

'Yahweh assayeth the righteous,
But the ungodly and him that loveth violence doth His soul hate.'

Ps. 20^8 (Heb. ^{9}):

'They are brought down and fallen,
But we are risen, and stand upright.'

This form of parallelism, which is not nearly so frequent in the Psalms as that first noticed, is specially characteristic of the Wisdom-literature, which, from the nature of the subjects with which it deals, naturally lends itself to this kind of contrasted thought. Instances are:

Prov. 10^1:

'A wise son maketh a glad father;
But a foolish son is the heaviness of his mother.'

Prov. 10^7:

'The memory of the just is blessed;
But the name of the wicked shall rot.

Prov. 15^{19}:

'The way of the sluggard is as an hedge of thorns;
But the path of the upright is made an highway.'

§ *Synthetic or Constructive Parallelism.*

In this form of parallelism the thought of the second line supplements and completes that of the first; there is parallelism, not in thought, but in *form* only. To quote the description of Lowth, 'word does not answer to word, and sentence to sentence, as equivalent or opposite; but there is a correspondence and equality between different propositions in respect of the shape and turn of the whole sentence, and of the constructive parts'.[1]

Ps. $3^{2,4}$ (Heb. ^{3,5}):

2. 'Many there be that say of my soul,
There is no help for him in his God.'

4. 'I did call upon Yahweh with my voice,
And He heard me out of His holy hill.'

Ps. 40^{1-3} (Heb. $^{2-4}$):

1. 'I waited patiently for Yahweh,
And He inclined unto me, and heard my cry;

2. And He brought me up out of the roaring pit, out of the miry clay,
And He set my feet upon a crag, He steadied my steps.

3. And He put a new song in my mouth,
Even praise to our God.
Many shall behold and fear,
And shall trust in Yahweh.'

[1] *Op. cit.*, p. xxi.

Prov. 6^{16-19}:

16\. 'These six things Yahweh hateth;
And seven are the abomination of His soul.

17\. Lofty eyes, a lying tongue,
And hands shedding innocent blood;

18\. A heart devising wicked thoughts,
Feet hasting to run unto mischief;

19\. A false witness breathing out lies,
And the sower of strife between brethren.'

The reason why we regard couplets of this character as parallel in *form* though not in *sense*, and instinctively class them as poetry and not plain prose, really lies in the fact that they are characterized by *identity of rhythm*. This introduces us to the second main characteristic of Hebrew poetry.

Rhythm.

We speak of a *rhythmical*, rather than of a *metrical*, system, because there seems to exist in Hebrew poetry no regularly quantitative system of metre (i. e. a strict form of scansion by feet consisting each of so many syllables in regular sequence), but rather a system of so many *ictûs* or rhythmical beats in each stichos, the number of intervening unstressed syllables being governed merely by the possibilities of pronunciation.

§ *Four-beat Rhythm.*

Three main varieties of rhythm are to be discerned in Hebrew poetry. The first which we shall notice consists of four beats to the verse-line, with a caesura in the middle which sometimes corresponds to a break in the sense, but at other times is purely formal. This rhythm, though common, is not so frequent as the three-beat rhythm which we shall notice later; but we place it first because it can be illustrated from Babylonian, where it is the ordinary rhythm in which the great epic poems are composed.

We will take an illustration from each of the two most famous Babylonian epics. The first comes from the Creation-myth (Tablet IV, ll. 93 ff.), and is a passage describing the battle between Marduk, the god of light, chosen champion of the gods, and Tiâmat, who represents primeval chaos (*Tiâmat* = Hebrew *T'hôm*, rendered 'the deep', i. e. the primeval abyss of waters, in Gen. 1[2]).

'Then there stoód forth Tiámat — and the gods' leáder Mardúk,
To the báttle they came ón, — they drew neár to the fíght.
Then the lórd threw wíde — his nét and enméshed her,
The húrricane that fóllowed him — befóre him he let loóse.
Then ópened her moúth — Tiámat to the utmóst;
The húrricane he drove ín, — that she coúld not close her líps;
With the míghty wínds — her bódy he fílled,
Her heárt was taken fróm her, — and her moúth she opened wíde.
He thréw the speár, — he sháttered her bódy,
Her ínwards he cut ópen, — he thrúst through her heárt.'

The second illustration is taken from the Gilgamesh epic (Tablet X, col. ii, ll. 21 ff.). Here the hero, in his search after the secret of immortality, reaches the shores of the western ocean, and inquires of a maiden named Siduri how he may cross to the far-distant island of the blessed, where dwells his ancestor Uta-napishtim (the Babylonian hero of the Flood), who has been raised by the gods to the rank of the immortals. Siduri replies,

'Néver, O Gílgamesh, a pássage hath there beén,
And nó one from etérnity hath cróssed the ócean.
The wárrior Shámash[1] hath cróssed the ócean;
But sáve for Shámash whó shall cróss?
Dífficult is the pássage, láborious its coúrse,
And deép are death's wáters that bár its áccess.
Whý, then, O Gílgamesh, wilt cróss the ócean?
At death's wáters when thou arrívest, whát wilt thou dó?'

This measure appears in Hebrew to be especially characteristic of poems which may be judged (upon other grounds) to be among the most ancient; and the influence of the Babylonian pattern may be conjectured to have been operative, or even a more remote tradition common to both peoples. We find it, e.g., in the song of triumph which celebrates the overthrow of the Egyptians in the Red Sea (Exod. 15), in the Song of Deborah (Judges 5), and in David's lament over Saul and Jonathan (2 Sam. 1^{19-27}). In all these examples it is not employed throughout, but alternates with another form of measure—that of three beats to the line.

[1] The Sun-god, who accomplishes the journey in his course through the ecliptic.

Cf. Exod. $15^{1,6}$:

'I will síng to Yahwéh,	for He hath triúmphed, hath triúmphed;
The hórse and his ríder	hath He whélmed in the seá.'

'Thy right hánd, O Yahwéh,	is glórious in pówer:
Thy right hánd, O Yahwéh,	doth shátter the foé.'

Judges 5^{3}:

'Atténd, ye kíngs;	give eár, ye rúlers:
Í—to Yahwéh	Í will síng,
Will make mélody to Yahwéh,	the Gód of Ísrael.'

2 Sam. 1^{22}:

'From the bloód of the slaín,	from the fát of the stróng
The bów of Jónathan	túrned not báck,
And the swórd of Saúl	retúrned not voíd.'

A good example of a Psalm composed throughout in this rhythm is Psalm 4.

2. 'When I cáll, O ánswer me,	Thou Gód of my ríght;
In distréss reliéve me,	and heár my práyer.
3. Sons of mén, how lóng	insúlt ye my hónour,
Lóving émptiness,	seéking untrúth?
4. Know thén that uníque	is Yahweh's kíndness to mé;
Yahwéh will heár	when I cáll unto Hím.

5.	Cómmune with your heárt	on your coúch, and be sílent;
6.	Óffer righteous sácrifices,	and trúst in Yahwéh.
7.	There be mány that sáy,	"Who can shów us goód?"
	O líft up upón us	the líght of Thy présence!
8.	O Yahwéh, Thou hast sét	fuller jóy in my heárt
	Than is theír's when their córn	and their múst aboúnd.
9.	In peáce will I bóth	lie dówn and sleép;
	For Thoú, Yahwéh,	mak'st me dwéll secúrely.'[1]

In the Prophets we may single out the magnificent chapter Isa. 33, as composed in the main in this rhythm. Cf. *vv.* [2–5]:

2.	'Fávour us, Yahwéh;	for Theé have we waíted:
	Be Thoú our árm	mórning by mórning,
	Yeá, our salvátion	in tíme of distréss.
3.	At the soúnd of the tumúlt	the peóples fléd,
	At Thy líftịng Thyself úp	the nátions were scáttered;

[1] Read in *v.* [2] Hebrew Text (R.V. *v.*[1]) Imperative הַרְחֶב־לִי, 'relieve me', in place of Perfect הִרְחַבְתָּ לִּי 'Thou hast relieved me' (unless this latter may be regarded as a Precative Perfect), and omit the rhythmically superfluous חָנֵּנִי, 'have mercy upon me'.

v. [4] Read חֶסֶד לִי (cf. Ps. 31^{22}) in place of חָסִיד לוֹ.

v. [5] Omit רִגְזוּ וְאַל תֶּחֱטָאוּ, 'Tremble and sin not', as outside the rhythmical scheme (possibly a marginal gloss upon Ps. 2^{11}).

v. [7] Take over יהוה at the end to the beginning of *v.* [8].

v. [9] Delete the rhythmically superfluous לְבָדָד, 'alone' (for which, if genuine, we should expect לְבַדֶּךָ), as dittography of לָבֶטַח, 'securely'.

4. And your spoíl shall be gáthered as the lócust gáthereth,
As grásshoppers leáp shall they leáp thereón.
5. Yahwéh is exálted, for He dwélleth on hígh;
He hath fíllèd Zión with júdgement and jústice.'

A specially fine passage is contained in *vv.* [13–16], and here the four-beat rhythm is varied by two three-beat couplets.

13. 'Heár, ye remóte ones, what Í have dóne;
And yé that are neár, acknówledge My míght.
14. The sínners in Zión are afraíd,
Trémbling hath seízed the gódless.
"Whó of us can dwéll with devoúring fíre?
Whó of us can dwéll with ceáseless búrnings?"
15. He that wálketh jústly, and speáketh upríghtly,
Scórneth the lúcre of ácts of fraúd,
Sháketh his hánd from clútching a bríbe,
Stóppeth his eár from heáring of bloód,
Clóseth his éyes from gázing on wróng.
16. Hé in the heíghts shall dwéll;
The stróngholds of the crágs shall be his fástness;
His breád shall be gíven, his wáters unfaíling.'

The four-beat Hebrew rhythm which these renderings aim at reproducing in English may be paralleled exactly in English poetry from *Piers Plowman*, where we have a similar variation in the number of unstressed syllables between the rhythmical beats. Compare the following passage which is cited by Dr. Buchanan Gray in his *Forms of Hebrew Poetry*, p. 130.

‘On Good Fríday I fýnde — a félon was y-sáved,
That had líved al his life — with lésynges and with théfte;
And for he béknede to the crós, — and to Chríst shrof hím,
He was sónner y-sáved — than seint Jóhan the Baptíst;
And or Ádam or Ysáye — or ány of the prophétes,
That hadde y-léyen with Lúcifer — mány long yéres.
A róbbere was y-raúnsoned — ráther than thei álle,
Withouten any pénaunce of púrgatorie — to perpétual blísse.’

Occasionally in Hebrew rhythm of this character we find parallelism, not between line and line of the couplets, but between the first and second halves of lines; and these should perhaps be reckoned, not as four-beat stichoi, but as couplets formed of short two-beat stichoi. This may be illustrated from Isa. 1^{4-6}:

4. ‘Ah! sínful ráce,
Folk láden with guílt,
Íll-doers’ seéd,
Degénerate sóns!
They have forsáken Yahwéh,
Despísed Israel’s Hóly One,
Gone báck estránged.
5. Whý be smitten stíll,
Ádding revólt?
Each heád is síck,
And each heárt diseásed.
6. From foót-sole to heád
No soúndness is thére;

Bruíse and weál
And féstering woúnd,
Unpréssed, unbándaged,
Unsóftened with oíntment.'

§ *Three-beat Rhythm.*

The second characteristic variety of Hebrew rhythm is that which contains three beats to the line. Three-beat couplets (with occasional triplets) are extremely frequent; numbers of the Psalms are so composed, and the Book of Job appears to exhibit this rhythm throughout. It is also frequent in the Prophets and in the Gnomic literature. As an example from the Psalms we may take Ps. 3:

2. 'Yahwéh, how mány are my foés,
Mány that ríse agaínst me,

3. Mány that sáy of my soúl,
"There is no hélp for hím in Gód".

4. But Thoú art a shiéld aboút me,
My glóry and the uplífter of my heád.

5. With my voíce to Yahwéh I criéd,
And He ánswered me from His hóly híll.

6. As for mé—I lay dówn and slépt;
I awóke, for Yahwéh sustaíns me.

7. I will not feár for mýriads of fólk
That are arráyed agaínst me round aboút.

8. Úp now! sáve me, O my Gód;
For Thou hast smítten all my énemies upon the cheék-bone,
The teéth of the wícked Thou hast sháttered.

9. Yahwéh's is the víctory:
On Thy fólk be Thy bléssing!'[1]

A very ancient fragment which may well be Davidic (or of David's age), embodied in Ps. 24, is cast in three-beat tristichs.

7. 'Líft up your heáds, O ye gátes,
And be lífted, ye áncient doórs,
That the Kíng of glóry may énter.

8. "Prithee whó is the Kíng of glóry?"
Yahwéh, the stróng and the váliant,
Yahwéh, the váliant in báttle.

9. Líft up your heáds, O ye gátes,
And be lífted, ye áncient doórs,
That the Kíng of glóry may énter.

10. "Prithee whó is the Kíng of glóry?"
Yahwéh, the Gód of hósts,
Hé is the Kíng of glóry.'[2]

The three-beat couplet is the rhythmical scheme of the Psalm which perhaps has the best claim to be considered Davidic (in the main)—Ps. 18, of which another recension is contained in 2 Sam. 22. The same rhythm (with an opening four-beat line) is found in perhaps the oldest poetic fragment of the Old Testament—the 'Song of the Sword', ascribed to Lamech in Gen. $4^{23,24}$, which evidently celebrates the invention or acquisition of weapons of bronze or iron by people in the nomadic stage:

23. 'Áda and Zílla, heár my voíce;
Wives of Lámech, give eár to my wórd:

[1] Omit יהוה in *v.* [4] and *v.* [8] Heb. Text (R.V. *vv.* [3, 7]).

[2] Insert אֱלֹהֵי before צְבָאוֹת in *v.* [10].

For a mán have I slaín for my woúnd,
And a bóy for the sáke of my bruíse:
24. If séven times Caín be avénged,
Then Lámech full séventy and séven.'

As a good example of this rhythm from the Prophets we may cite the well-known passage in Mic. 6^{6-8}:

6. 'Wherewíth shall I meét Yahwéh,
Bow dówn to the Gód of the heíght?
Shấll I go to meét Him with burnt-ófferings,
With cálves of yeárling grówth?
7. Will Yahwéh be pleásed with thoúsands of ráms,
With mýriads of rívers of oíl?
Shall I gíve my fírstborn for my faúlt,
Body's fruít for the sín of my soúl?
8. He hath declắred unto theé, O mán, what is goód;
And whắt doth Yahwéh seek fróm thee,
But dóing of jústice and lóving of kíndness,
And húmbly to wálk with thy Gód?'

Here we notice the occurrence of three four-beat lines which form a pleasing variation.

Another illustration may be drawn from Isa. $51^{7,8}$:

7. 'Hárk to Me, yé that know ríghteousness,
Fólk in whose heárt is My láw;
Feár not reproách of frail mén,
And bé not borne dówn by their scóffs.
8. For the móth shall eát them like a róbe,
And the wórm shall eát them like woól;
But My ríghteousness lásteth for áye,
And My salvátion to áge upon áge.'

The whole section formed by *vv.* $^{1-8}$ of this chapter is a poem cast in this rhythm.

Not infrequently four-beat rhythm and three-beat rhythm are combined in a single composition. A fine illustration of this is Ps. 46, which falls into three stanzas containing, as a rule, four rhythmical beats to the line, varied by couplets of three beats to the line which mark the close of each stanza.

2. 'Gód is for ús   a réfuge and stréngth,
A hélp in troúbles   króved full wéll:
3. Therefóre fear we nót   though the eárth be móved,
Though the moúntains subsíde   in the heárt of the seá.
4. Its wáters ráge and foám;
The moúntains quáke at its swélling.

5. There's a ríver whose streáms   make glád God's cíty;
By thém the Most Hígh   has hállowed His abóde.
6. Gód is in her mídst,   she shall nót be móved;
Gód shall hélp her   at the túrn of the mórning.
7. Nátions roár,   kíngdoms sháke;
He útters His voíce,   the eárth dissólves.
8. The Lórd of hósts is wíth us;
Our strónghold is Jácob's Gód.

9. Cóme, behóld   the wórks of Yahwéh,
Hów He has sét   dismáy on the eárth:
10. Abólishing wárs   to the boúnds of the eárth,
The bów He breáks,   and snáps the speár,
The wággons He búrns in the fíre.
11. Desíst and knów   that Í am Gód;
I will be exálted among the nátions,   I will be exálted in the eárth.

12. The Lórd of hósts is wíth us;
Our strónghold is Jácob's Gód.'[1]

The same combination of rhythms may be illustrated from the opening of the 'Song of Deborah', Judges 5^{3-5}:

3. 'Atténd, ye kíngs; give eár, ye rúlers:
Í—to Yahwéh Í will síng,
Will make mélody the Gód of Ísrael.
to Yahwéh,

4. Yahwéh, in Thy prógress from Seír,
In Thy márch from the fiéld of Edóm,
Eárth quáked, yea, heáven rócked,
Yea, the cloúds drópped wáter.

5. The moúntains shoók before Yahwéh,
Befóre Yahwéh, the Gód of Ísrael.'[2]

[1] In *v.* [5b] (R.V. *v.* [4b]) the Massoretic Text offers the somewhat strange expression קְדֹשׁ מִשְׁכְּנֵי עֶלְיוֹן, 'The holy place of the tabernacles of the Most High', in place of which LXX reads, *ἡγίασεν τὸ σκήνωμα αὐτοῦ ὁ ὕψιστος*, i. e. קִדֵּשׁ מִשְׁכָּנוֹ עֶלְיוֹן—superior to the accepted text, but, like it, offering only three rhythmical stresses, and somewhat abrupt in its disconnexion from the preceding line. We gain a fourth stress accent and improve the connexion by supplying אֲלֵיהֶם, 'By them' (the streams) at the beginning, which may have accidentally dropped out owing to its resemblance to אֱלֹהִים, 'God', preceding. In *v.* [6] לִפְנוֹת בֹּקֶר would naturally carry one stress only, the accent on *lipnṓt* being annulled before that on *bṓḳer* (cf. p. 44). Very possibly, however, the original reading may have been *lipnṓt habbṓḳer*. If *v.* [9b] is really a four-stress line, we must suppose that the relative אֲשֶׁר carries a stress immediately before the stress on שָׂם, with which it is so closely connected; but this would be contrary to the general rule, and it is denied by the Massoretes through their connexion of the two words by *Maḳḳēph*. Conceivably the line may have begun with הָאֵל, 'The God' (parallel to 'Yahweh' in the preceding line):—

hā'ḗl 'ᵃšer sā́m | šammṓt bā'ā́reṣ

'The Gód who has sét | dismáy on the éarth.'

[2] In the last line of *v.* [5] the Massoretic text contains the gloss זֶה סִינַי, 'This is Sinai'—originally a marginal comment explaining

Another occasional combination, not infrequent in the Book of Proverbs, is a couplet in which a four-beat line is followed by one of three beats.

§ *Ḳīnā-rhythm.*

We now pass on to a third and very striking form of Hebrew rhythm in which the verse-line falls into two parts of unequal length. The first part normally contains three stresses, though variations of four or two stresses are permissible; the second part regularly contains two stresses only. In cases in which the first half offers only two stresses, the effect of greater length than that of the second two-stressed half is conveyed by the use of longer or weightier words. Thus we have a limping measure in which the second half of the line seems to form an echo of the first, the effect being peculiarly plaintive and touching. This measure is characteristic of the *Ḳīnā* or dirge, and is often described as *Ḳīnā*-rhythm. It is not, however, confined to the dirge, but is often used in other forms of poetry which express keen emotion, whether the emotion be produced by sorrow or by the kind of joy which is not far removed from tears.

An example of a short dirge described as a *Ḳīnā* is found in Amos 5[2]:

'She is fállen, no móre shall she ríse,
the vírgin of Ísrael;
Forsáken on her soíl,
nóne to upraíse her.'

Here in the second line, which runs in Hebrew

niṭṭ^ešá 'al 'admāṭáh
'ḗn meḳīmáh,

the reference to the mountains shaking. The words spoil the rhythm, and can be no part of the original text.

the first half seems to contain two stresses only,[1] but is evidently more weighty than the two-stressed second half.

As might be expected, this rhythm characterizes the Book of Lamentations, being found in the first four chapters, though not in the fifth. A good illustration of it may be chosen from the opening of chapter 3, which is an alphabetical poem in groups of three verses, the first three beginning with א, the second three with ב, and so forth.

1. 'Í am the mán that hath seén afflíction
by the ród of His wráth.
2. Mé hath He léd and condúcted
in dárkness, nót líght.
3. Against mé doth He cónstantly túrn
His hánd all day lóng.

4. He hath wórn out my flésh and my skín,
He hath bróken my bónes.
5. He hath buílded and cómpassed me roúnd
with gáll and travaíl.
6. In gloómy pláces hath He stáblished me,
like the deád of old tíme.

7. He hath fénced me roúnd beyond escápe,
He hath weíghted my chaín.
8. Yeá, though I cáll and cry oút,
He exclúdeth my práyer.
9. He hath fénced my wáys with hewn stóne,
my páths hath He twísted.'

The question may be raised whether these 3 (4, 2) beat + 2 beat lines are to be regarded as couplets formed of two lines of unequal length, or whether they are not rather to be viewed as long 5 (6, 4) beat lines

[1] Cf., however, the discussion on pp. 50, 51.

divided unequally by a strongly marked caesura. In the passage quoted from Lamentations it may be noticed that in *vv.* [4,7,9] the two parts of the verse present the characteristics of mutual parallelism, while in *vv.* [1,2,3,5,6,8] the sense runs on from the first half into the second, in most cases without a break which can be represented in English even by a comma. It may be held that the question is settled in favour of the theory of a long single line with caesura by the fact that in many poems the whole 3 + 2 stress line is manifestly parallel with the like period which succeeds it, either synonymously or in the relation which we have described as synthetic. This is plainly seen in Ps. 27^{1-6}, which seems originally to have formed a complete poem by itself.

1. 'Yahwéh is my líght and my salvátion;
   whóm shall I feár?
   Yahwéh is the strónghold of my lífe;
   whóm shall I dreád?
2. When evildóers drew nígh agaínst me
   to eát my flésh,
   My ádversaries and my énemies, e'en míne,
   'twas théy that stúmbled.
3. Though a hóst should encámp agaínst me,
   my heárt would not feár;
   Though wár should aríse agaínst me,
   yét would I be tránquil.
4. Óne thing have I ásked of Yahwéh;
   thát will I seék:
   To dwéll in the hoúse of Yahwéh
   all the dáys of my lífe;
   To gáze on the lóveliness of Yahwéh,
   and to enquíre in His témple.

5. For He treásures me in His cóvert
in the dáy of troúble;
He hídes me in the híding of His tént;
on a crág He sets me hígh.
6. And nów shall He raíse up my heád
o'er my foés round aboút me;
And I will sácrifice sácrifices of tríumph,
I will síng and make mélody.'[1]

Here we have three distichs followed by a tristich and two distichs. In the first, third, and fourth distichs the parallelism is synonymous, in the second and fifth synthetic, and this is also the case in the tristich. A similar arrangement of the 3 + 2 stress lines in couplets is to be observed in Ps. 5:

2. 'Give eár to my wórds, Yahwéh,
detéct my whísper;
3. Atténd to the soúnd of my crý,
my Kíng and my Gód.
4. Unto Theé will I práy, Yahwéh,
for Thou wilt heár my voíce;
In the mórning will I set fórth my burnt-óffering,
and will wátch for Thy wórd.
5. No Gód willing évil art Thoú;
wrong may nót be Thy guést.
6. Brággarts may nót take their stánd
in síght of Thine éyes.
Thou hátest all wórkers of évil,
7. the speákers of liés;
The mán of bloódshed and deceít
Yahwéh abhórs.

[1] Omitting ונפלו, 'and fell', in *v.* 2 b, and באהלו, 'in his tent', ליהוה, 'to Yahweh', in *v.* 6 b.

8. But Í, through the weálth of Thy kíndness,
may énter Thy hoúse,
May bów t'ward Thy hóly pálace
in áwe of Theé.

9. Leád me, Yahwéh, in Thy ríghteousness,
becaúse of mine énemies;
Make straíght my wáy befóre me,
⟨by reáson of mine ádversaries.⟩

10. For naúght is steádfast in their moúth;
their heárt is an abýss:
Their throát is an ópen gráve;
their tóngue they make smoóth.

11. Condémn them, O Gód; let them fáll
through their ówn devíces;
For the múltitude of their crímes thrust them dówn,
for they rebél against Theé.

12. And let áll Thy depéndants rejoíce;
for éver let them síng:
And let the lóvers of Thy náme exult in Theé,
because Thoú deféndest them.

13. Thou wilt bléss the ríghteous, Yahwéh;
with fávour wilt Thou surroúnd
him.'[1]

[1] *vv.* ^{3b}, ^{4a}. כי אליך אתפלל: יהוה בקר תשמע קולי should form one *Ḳīnā*-verse (*v.* ^{4a}), which is gained by reading כי | אליך אתפלל יהוה חשמע קולי (בקר dittography from *v.* ^{4b}).

v. ^{4b} is assumed to have formed the next *Ḳīnā*-verse, in the form בֹּקֶר אֶעֱרָךְ עֹלָתֶךָ | וַאֲצַפֶּה דְבָרֶךָ׃ (לך a remnant of עולתך, and כי at the beginning of *v.* ^{5} a remnant of דברך). For the final phrase, 'and I will watch for thy word', cf. Hab. 2^{1} וַאֲצַפֶּה לִרְאוֹת מַה־יְדַבֶּר־בִּי, 'and I will watch to see what He will speak with me'; Num. 23^{3-5}.

vv. ^{6b}, ^{7a}, should form a *Ḳīnā*-verse, and this is gained by omission of תְּאַבֵּד, 'Thou wilt destroy'.

v. ^{9b}. The two-stress second member of the *Ḳīnā*-verse is wanting,

Here we observe, in *v.* [11a]:

'Condémn them, O Gód; let them fáll
through their ówn devíces,'

a case in which the rhythmical caesura is so purely formal that it ignores the sense-division (on 'God') and falls where there is a sense-connexion. This, though uncommon, can be paralleled from other poems where the rhythmical structure is clearly marked and the text not to be suspected of corruption. Compare the second line of the following couplet from the fine 'Taunt-song' against the King of Babylon in Isa. 14 (*v.* [8]):

'Yea, the fír-trees rejoíce at thy fáte,
the cédars of Lébanon;
"Since thoú art laíd low, comes not úp
the héwer agaínst us".'

The case is similar in Lam. 3[12]:

'He has bént His bów, and sét me
as a márk for the árrow.'

An example of a dirge, composed in the *Ḳīnā*-rhythm

and this is conjecturally supplied by מִפְּנֵי צָרָי, as a parallel to לְמַעַן שׁוֹרְרָי in *v.* [9a].

v. [10a]. בְּפִיהוּ, 'in his mouth', is corrected to בְּפִימוֹ, 'in their mouth', in accordance with the plurals of *v.* [9], *v.* [10b].

v. [12b]. A transposition seems to have taken place, the short member coming first. This is corrected, reading כִּי תָסֵךְ for וְתָסֵךְ.

v. [13]. Omit כִּי־אַתָּה, 'For Thou', and כַּצִּנָּה, 'as with a shield', as corrupt dittography of רָצוֹן, '(with) favour'.

These corrections, though considerable, seem to be justified by the fact that they restore in six verses the rhythm which is elsewhere found with perfect regularity in thirteen *Ḳīnā*-verses. The rendering of *v.* [12] 'áll Thy depéndants' for *kol ḥōsē bāk*, properly 'all that take refuge in Thee', is adopted in order to reproduce the rhythm of the original.

and introduced by the characteristic opening *'ēkā* 'How?'[1]—may be seen in Isa. 1^{21-23}:

21. 'Hów hath she becóme a hárlot,
the cíty once-faíthful;
Zión that was fúll of jústice,
ríghteousness lódged there?
22. Thy sílver hath becóme dróss,
thy wíne dilúted;
23. Thy prínces have becóme rebéllious,
and cómrades of thiéves.
Éveryone lóveth a bríbe,
and pursúeth rewárds;
The caúse of the wídow they pleád not,
the órphan they ríght not.'[2]

In the same chapter, *vv.* $^{10-17}$, the rhythm is used in an indictment of religious formality:

10. 'Heár the wórd of Yahwéh,
Ye chiéftains of Sódom;
Give eár to the instrúction of our Gód,
ye fólk of Gomórrah.
11. What to Mé the hóst of your sacrifíces?
saíth Yahwéh.
I am sáted with burnt-ófferings of ráms,
and fát of fed beásts;
And the bloód of búlls and lámbs
and he-goáts I desíre not.

[1] אֵיכָה is similarly employed in the opening of dirges composed in this rhythm in Jer. 48^{17}, Lam. 1^1, 2^1, 4^1.

[2] In *v.* $^{21\,b}$ צִיּוֹן (derived from LXX) is supplied at the beginning of the line, and the final words וְעַתָּה מְרַצְּחִים, 'but now murderers', are deleted as a gloss. In *v.* ^{22} בַּמָּיִם, 'with water', is deleted. In *v.* $^{23\,a}$ הָיוּ, 'have become', is supplied to fill out the line (cf. הָיְתָה in *v.* ^{22}). In *v.* $^{23\,b}$ an accidental transposition of clauses seems to have taken place, and the restored text reads ריב אלמנה לא יריבו | יתום לא ישפטו.

12. When ye cóme to seé my fáce,
who hath asked thís?

13. Trámple my coúrts no móre,
nor bríng vain gíft;
Sweet smóke is to Mé an abhórrence,
yea, new moón and Sábbath;
The cálling of assémbly I cannot beár,
yea, fást and solémnity.

14. Your new moóns and your státed feásts
My soúl detésts;
They are becóme a búrden upón Me,
I am weáry of beáring.

15. And whén ye stretch fórth your hánds,
I will híde my éyes,
Yeá, though ye múltiply práyer,
I wíll not heár.
Your hánds are fúll of bloódshed;
16. wásh you, make you cleán;
Remóve the évil of your dóings
from befóre my éyes.
Ceáse to do évil;
17. Leárn to do góod;
Seék out jústice;
Chastíse the rúthless;
Ríght the órphan;
Pleád for the wídow.'[1]

[1] This rendering involves omission of מִיֶּדְכֶם, 'at your hand', in *v.* [12], and of מִכֶּם, 'from you', in *v.* [15]. רמם חצרי at the end of *v.* [12] is connected with *v.* [13], and ידיכם דמים מלאו at the end of *v.* [15] with *v.* [16]. We vocalize לִרְאוֹת פָּנָי, 'to see My face', in *v.* [12], in place of לֵרָאוֹת פָּנָי, 'to be seen of My face', i.e. 'to appear before Me' (a Massoretic alteration regularly made in order to remove an expression offensive to later thought); and emend אָוֶן, 'iniquity', to צוֹם, 'fast' (with LXX), in *v.* [13], and אַשְּׁרוּ, 'right', to יַסְּרוּ, 'chastise', in *v.* [17].

As an example of variation in the number of stresses in the first half-verse of a *Ḳīnā*-poem we may quote Isa. 51[17–20]:

17. 'Aroúse thyself, aroúse thyself,
stand úp, Jerúsalem!
Who hast drúnk at the hánd of Yahwéh
the cúp of His wráth;
The bówl of the cúp of reẹ́ling
thou hast drúnk, hast draíned.

18. There is nóne that leádeth her
of all the chíldren she hath bórne;
And there is nóne that hóldeth her hánd
of all the chíldren she hath reáred.

19. Twó things are théy which shall befáll thee;
whó shall bemoán thee?
Desolátion, and destrúction, and the fámine, and the swórd;
whó shall cómfort thee?[1]

20. Thy sóns have faínted; they lié at the tóp of all the streéts
like an ántelope in a nét;
Fúll of the wráth of Yahwéh,
the rebúke of thy Gód.'[1]

Here the first members of the *Ḳīnā*-verses in *vv.* [17a, 18a] have two stresses only, while that of *v.* [19b] has four, and that of *v.* [20] as many as five. Some scholars (Duhm, Cheyne, Marti, Box) would lighten this last line by omission of the words 'at the top of all the streets' as a gloss-citation from Lam. 2[19]; but this is scarcely necessary. The rhythm—owing doubtless to the regularity of the two-stressed second members of

[1] Reading in *v.* [19b] the 3rd pers. מִי יְנַחֲמֵךְ (with the ancient Versions), in place of 1st pers. אֲנַחֲמֵךְ, which is strange after מִי.

the verses—rings true, and the variation in the length of the first members adds, if anything, to the emotional quality of the poetry.

The Principles of Stress-accentuation in Hebrew Poetry.

Before leaving the subject of Hebrew rhythm, it seems worth while to formulate the rules which have been applied in determining the rhythmical character of all passages which have come under consideration. Such formulation is desirable, not merely as a justification of the rhythmical schemes which have been set forth, but also as a self-discipline; for, while detection of the fact that the poetry of the Old Testament is rhythmical is (or should be) instinctive to the Hebrew scholar, the fact that this rhythm must be governed by more or less definite rules is not equally recognized; and we thus sometimes find scholars forcing passages into a preconceived scheme of rhythm which will hardly bear the test of close examination.

In speaking of 'rules', we mean instinctive, rather than cut-and-dried, rules; for it is clear that the prime test of rhythm is the natural appeal that it makes to the ear. Coming, however, as we do, at the subject from the outside, and not as born Hebrew poets, it should be possible to discipline the instinct and aid the ear by formulating certain main rules of Hebrew rhythm as they may be gathered from passages in which the scheme appears to be well marked and the text preserved substantially in its original form. The following rules are based upon the examples which have been given in this chapter—a plan which has the advantage of dealing with a limited though sufficiently wide basis of material; and the endeavour has been made to account, so far as may be, for all rhythmical phenomena which arise within this compass.[1]

§ 1. Every word, with the exception of monosyllabic particles, normally receives one stress-accent. Thus Exod. 15[6]:

yᵉmīnᵉkā́ Yahwéh | *neʼdārī́ bakkṓᵃḥ*
yᵉmīnᵉkā́ Yahwéh | *tirʻáṣ ʼōyḗb*

'Thy right hánd, O Yahwéh, | is glórious in pówer;
Thy right hánd, O Yahwéh, | doth shátter the foé.'

§ 2. The occurrence of two stress-accents in immediate connexion, without a caesura or break in sense between them involving a pause, would be uneuphonious; thus the stress which a word accented on the ultimate would normally bear is annulled if the closely connected word following bears an accent on the first syllable. So

Gen. 4[23]: *nᵉšē Lémek*, 'wives of Lámech' (not *nᵉšḗ Lémek*).

Isa. 1[4]: *hōy gṓy ḥōṭḗ* | *ʻam kébed ʻāwṓn*
'Ah, sínful ráce, | folk láden with guílt!'

Here *hōy*, 'Ah!' and *ʻam*, 'folk', lose their stress owing to the stress immediately following.

[1] We have assumed the licence of correcting the position of the accent in the Massoretic Text in cases in which two tone-syllables would come together without a break in connexion, and the first is capable of retraction, according to existing rule, on to an open syllable preceding. Thus in Amos 5[2] the Massoretes offer the rhythmically intolerable *lō-tōsī́ph ḳū́m*; but we may justly suppose that the accentuation really intended is *lō-tṓseph ḳū́m*. In such cases, however, the Massoretic vocalization has been retained (e.g. we have written *tṓsīph*; not *tṓseph*), because it would lie somewhat outside our province in the present connexion to theorize as to the vocal-changes which might be induced by such retraction.

Isa. 1^5: *'al mé tukkū 'ṓd*, 'Whý be smitten stíll?'

Isa. 1^6:

mikkaph régel we'ad rṓš | *'ēn bṓ meṭṓm*
'From foót-sole to heád | not ín-it (is) soúndness.'

Isa. 1^{13}: *minḥat šā́w*, 'vain gíft' (lit. 'gift of vanity').

Ps. 4^3: *bₑnē 'ī́š*, 'Sons of mén'; *v.* 6: *zibḥū́ zibḥē ṣédeḳ*, 'Óffer righteous sacrifíces' (lit. 'sacrifices of righteousness').

§ 3. There seems, however, to be no objection to the immediate sequence of one stress-accent by another if a marked pause intervenes.

Such a pause may be formed by a caesura which halves a four-stress stichos.

Isa. 33^4:

we'ussáph šelalkém | *'ṓseph heḥāsī́l*
kemaššā́ḳ gēbī́m | *šṓḳēḳ bṓ*

i.e. literally rendered,

'And shall be gáthered your spoíl, | gáthering of the lócust,
Like leáping of grass-hóppers, | leáping thereón.'

Ps. 46^6: *'elōhī́m beḳirbā́h* | *bál timmṓṭ*
'Gód is in her mídst; | ne'ér shall she be móved.'

Ps. 46^7: *hāmū́ gōyī́m* | *mā́ṭu mamlākṓt*
nātā́n beḳōlṓ | *tā́mūg 'ā́reṣ*
'Nátions roár, | kíngdoms sháke;
He útters His voíce, | eárth dissólves.'

In three-stress rhythm, where there is no clearly marked caesura, two stress-accents may occur together where there is a disjunctive accent, marking a slight pause, between them.

Ps. $24^{7, 9}$: *weyābṓ mélek hakkābṓd*
'That may énter, the Kíng of glóry.'

Ps. 24^{10}: *hū́ mélek hakkābṓd*

'Hé (is) the Kíng of glóry'.

§ 4. The stress-accent of a word accented on the first syllable does not annul the accent of a closely connected word preceding which normally would be accented on the ultimate, if the penultimate syllable of this preceding word contains a long vowel in an open syllable, or a short vowel in a half-open syllable (as distinct from a short vowel in a closed syllable). In such a case, the stress-accent is thrown back on the penultimate syllable.

Isa. 1^{23}: *kullṓ 'ṓhēb šṓḥad*

'Everyóne lóveth a bríbe'.

Normal accent *'ōhḗb*. Since *kullṓ* bears a distinctive accent, i.e. since there is a felt break between it and *'ṓhēb* in contrast to the close connexion in which *'ṓhēb* stands to *šṓḥad*, there is no objection to the accent of *'ṓhēb* following immediately upon that of *kullṓ*.

Isa. 33^{4}: *k^e^maššáḳ gēbī́m | šṓḳēḳ bṓ*

'Like leáping of grass- | leáping thereón'.
hóppers,

Normal accent *šōḳḗḳ*.

Isa. 51^{8}: *kī kabbéged yṓk^e^lēm 'ā́š*

'For like a gárment, shall eát them the móth'.

Normal accent *yōk^e^lḗm*.

Amos 5^{2}: *lō-tṓsīph ḳū́m*

'No móre shall she ríse'.

Normal accent *tōsī́ph*.

Micah 6^{7}: *b^e^ríb^e^bōt náḥ^a^lē šā́men*

'With mýriads of rívers of oíl'.

The normal accent of *naḥ^a^lḗ* is retracted before *šā́men*, and this in turn causes the retraction of the normal accent of *b^e^rib^e^bṓt*.

Ps. 3^{7}: *lō 'īrā́ merib*ᵉ*bōt 'ā́m*

'I will not feár for mýriads of fólk'.

Ps. 3^{8}: *kī hikkī́tā 'et kol 'óy*ᵉ*bay léḥī*

'For Thou hast smítten all my énemies upon the cheék-bone'.

Normal accent *'ōy*ᵉ*báy.*

Ps. 4^{8}: *mē'ḗt d*ᵉ*gānā́m* | *w*ᵉ*tīrṓšām rā́bbū*

'More than (in) the tíme | and their múst aboúnd'.
when their córn

Normal accent *w*ᵉ*tī́rōšā́m.*

Ps. 5^{6}: *sānḗtā kol pṓ'ᵃlē 'ā́wen*

'Thou hátest all wórkers of évil'.

Normal accent *pō'ᵃlḗ.*

Ps. 5^{12}: *w*ᵉ*yism*ᵉ*ḥū́ kol ḥōsē bā́k*

'And let áll Thy depéndants[1] rejoíce'.

Normal accent *ḥōsḗ.*

Ps. 27^{2}: *ṣāráy w*ᵉ*'ṓy*ᵉ*bay lī́*

'Mine ádversaries and my énemies, e'en míne'.

Whether the stress-accent was ever thrown back upon *a closed syllable* is very questionable. In Gen. 4^{24} we find in the Massoretic text יֻקַּם־קָיִן—an accentuation which, by the use of *Maḳḳēph* and the marking of a countertone on the sharpened syllable of יֻקַּם, gives the triple stressing of the line as follows:

kī šib'ātáyim yúḳḳam Ḳā́yin

'If séven times Caín be avénged'.

A few similar cases are collected by G.–K., § 29*g*, but they are extremely rare; and it seems clear that such a proceeding, if ever really practised, was at any rate highly irregular. It is not improbable that the

[1] Lit. 'all they that take refuge in Thee'. The rendering given above is adopted for the sake of rhythm.

particle *kī*, 'If', was intended to take the first stress, and *yuḳḳam* to lose its stress before *Ḳáyin*:

kí šib'ātáyim yuḳḳam Ḳáyin.

§ 5 (*a*). A word which contains a long vowel two places before the stress-accent, i. e. with one full vowel intervening (or, it may be, one half-vowel and one full vowel), takes a countertone on this long vowel (marked with *Methegh* by the Massoretes), which normally counts as an additional stress-accent.

Gen. 4^{23}: *lᵉḥabbúrātí*, 'for my bruise' (rendered 'for the sáke of my bruíse' on p. 31, to reproduce the two stress-accents).

Isa. 1^{14}: *ḥodšēkém ūmṓ'ᵃdēkém*
'Your-new-moóns and-your-státed-feásts'.

Isa. 33^{2}: *'aph yᵉšū́'ātḗnū* | *bᵉ'ḗt ṣará*
'Yeá, our salvátion | in tíme of distréss'.

Reproduction in English involves one stress on 'yea' and one on 'salvation', but in Hebrew *'aph* = 'yea' is unstressed and two stresses fall on *yᵉšū́'ātḗnū*, 'our salvation'.

Isa. 33^{3}: *mērṓmᵉmūtékā* | *nāphᵉṣū́ gōyī́m*
'At-Thy-lífting-Thyself-úp | the-nátions were-scáttered'.

Isa. 33^{13}: *ūdᵉ'ū́ ḳᵉrōbī́m* | *gᵉbū́rātī́*
'And-acknówledge, ye-neár-ones, | My-wárlike-míght'.

Isa. 51^{7}: *ūmiggiddū́phōtám al tēḥáttū*
'And-by-their-scóffing-wórds be not dismáyed'.

(*b*) A short vowel in a half-open syllable two places before the stress-accent seems frequently to carry a second stress-accent.

Isa. 33^{15}: *mōʻēs b^{e}béṣaʻ* | *máʻ^{a}šaḳḳōt*
'That-scórneth the-lúcre | of-ácts-of-fraúd'.

Micah 6^{6}: *háʻ^{a}ḳadd^{e}ménnu b^{e}ʻōlṓt*
'Shálll-I-go-to-meét-Him with-burnt-ófferings?'

Lam. 3^{6}: *b^{e}máḥ^{a}šakkīm hōšībánī*
'In-gloómy-pláces hath-He-stáblished-me'.

N.B. This rule is not, however, of universal application. Cases can be collected in which a word containing a long vowel two places from the tone is clearly only intended to carry one stress-accent, the countertone being neglected.

Isa. 51^{8}: *w^{e}ṣidḳātī́ l^{e}ʻōlám tihyé*
wīšūʻātī́ l^{e}dṓr dōrī́m
'But-My-ríghteousness lásteth for-áye,
And-My-salvátion to-áge upon-áge'.

Here the fact that *wīšūʻātī́*, 'and My salvátion', carries one stress only (not *wī́šūʻātī́*) is perhaps due to a sense of its correspondence with the parallel *w^{e}ṣidkātī́*, 'and My righteousness'.

2 Sam. 1^{22}:
ḳéšet Y^{e}hōnātán | *lō nāsṓg 'āḥṓr*
w^{e}ḥéreb Šāʼū́l | *lō tāšū́b rēḳám*
'The bów of Jónathan | túrned not báck,
And the swórd of Saúl | retúrned not voíd'.

Ps. 4^{9}: *kī 'attā́ Yahwéh* | *lābéṭaḥ tōšībḗnī*
'For Thoú, Yahwéh, | mak'st me dwéll secúrely'.

In these two instances the neglect of the countertone in *Y^{e}hṓnātán*, *tṓšībḗnī* may be due to the fact that both words are preceded by a Segholate noun in which the unaccented helping vowel was probably very slightly heard, if heard at all, the combinations being pronounced *ḳéšt Yōnatán*, *lābéṭḥ tōšībḗnī*. Thus the preceding accentual stress may well have annulled the stress of the countertone (cf. § 6 *a*).

Neglect of the stress of the countertone may frequently be seen in the short two-stress member of a *Ḳīnā*-verse.

Lam. 3[9]:

nᵉtībōtáy ʿiwwā́, 'My páths hath He twísted'.

v. [14]: *ᵉngīnātā́m kol hayyṓm*, 'Their sóng all day lóng'.

v. [18]: *wᵉtōḥaltī́ mē Yahwéh*, 'And my expectátion from Yahwéh'.

v. [23]: *rabbā́ ʾᵉmūnātékā*, 'Greát is Thy faíthfulness'.

Ps. 27[4]:

lᵉbaḳḳḗr bᵉhēkālṓ, 'and to inquíre in His témple'.

v. [6]: *ʿal ʾōyᵉbáy sᵉbībōtáy*, 'O'er my foés round aboút me'.

(*c*) Whether *a closed syllable* two places from the tone ever carries a second stress-accent is questionable. The Massoretes do not, in such a case, mark a countertone by the use of *Methegh*. It is, at any rate, a significant fact that out of all the passages which have been taken in this chapter as illustrations of Hebrew rhythm, and from which the principles which govern the stress are drawn, the cases which come up for consideration are very few, and may be susceptible of another explanation.

Amos 5[2]: *niṭṭᵉšā́ ʿal ʾadmātā́h*

'She is forsáken on her soíl'.

Lam. 3[15]: *hisbīʿánī bammᵉrōrī́m*

'He hath sáted me with bítterness'.

Both these passages are the first halves of a *Ḳīnā*-verse, which normally contain three stresses, and in reading them it is natural to stress *ʿalʾádmātā́h, bámmᵉrōrī́m*. It may be, however, that they are properly to be reckoned two-stress lines, the contrast with the short two-stress member which follows being secured by the use of more lengthy words (cf. p. 35). An illustration of this is to be seen in Ps. 27[5] *kī yiṣpᵉnḗnī bᵉsukkṓ*, 'For He treásures me in His cóver'—unless, as is possible, the conjunction *kī* is intended to carry a stress.

Isa. 33[2]: *hᵉyḗ zᵉrōʿā́m* | *lábbᵉḳārī́m*

'Be Thoú their árm | mórning by mórning'.

If the four-stress rhythm which characterizes this chapter is here illustrated, *labbᵉḳārīm* must bear two stresses. Elsewhere in the poem, however, we find occasional three-stress couplets, e.g. *vv.* [14a, 16a] (cf. p. 27); and in *v.*[17] we seem to have a couplet of 4 + 3 stresses:

mélek bᵉyophyṓ | *teḥᵉzénā ʿēnékā*
tirʾéna ʾéreṣ marḥaḳḳī́m

'The kíng in his beáuty | thine éyes shall seé;
They shall béhold a fár-stretching lánd'.

Thus *v.*[2b] may be intended for a 3 + 4 stress couplet:

hᵉyḗ zᵉrōʿā́m labbᵉḳārī́m
ʾaph yᵉšūʿā́tḗnū | *bᵉʿḗt ṣārā́.*

Ps. 5[8]:

ʾeštaḥᵃwéʾel hēkā́l ḳodšékā | *bᵉyírʾātékā*

'I will bow dówn to | in áwe of Theé'.
Thy hóly pálace,

Here it seems clear that *bᵉyirʾātekā*, as the second *Ḳīnā*-member, must be intended to bear two stresses.

If we go outside the special passages to which we have limited our examination, it is possible to cite evidence that in some forms of poetry a closed syllable two places from the tone carries a stress-accent. This is evident in the following passage from Ecclus. 38[16–23], where the four-stress rhythm is very well marked.

16.	*bᵉnī́ ʿal hammḗt*	*hāzḗb dimʿā́*
	hítmārḗr	*ūnᵉhḗ ḳīnā́*
	kᵉmíšpāṭṓ	*ʾᵉsṓph šᵉʾērṓ*
	wᵉʾal títʿallḗm	*bigwīʿātṓ*
17.	*hāmḗr bᵉkī́*	*wᵉhāḥḗm mispḗd*
	wᵉšī́t ʾeblṓ	*kᵉyṓṣē bṓ*
	yṓm ūšᵉnáyim	*baʿᵃbū́r dimʿā́*
	wᵉhínnāḥḗm	*baʿᵃbū́r dāwṓn*
18.	*míddāwṓn*	*yōṣḗ ʾāsṓn*
	kēn rṓᵃʿ lēbā́b	*yibné ʿᵃṣībā́*
20.	*ʾál tāšḗb*	*ʾēlā́w lēb ʿṓd*
	pᵉráʿ zikrṓ	*ūzᵉkṓr ʾaḥᵃrī́t*
21.	*ʾál tizkᵉrḗhū*	*kī ʾēn lṓ tiḳwā́*
	mát-tōʿī́l	*ūlᵉkā́ tārḗᵃʿ*
22.	*zᵉkṓr ḥuḳḳṓ*	*kī hū́ ḥuḳḳékā*
	lṓ ʾetmṓl	*ūlᵉkā́ hayyṓm*
23.	*kíšbōt mḗt*	*yišbṓt zikrṓ*
	hínnāḥḗm	*ʿim ṣḗt naphšṓ*[1]

16.	'My són, for the deád	let fáll a teár,
	Afflíct thysélf	and lamént with a dírge.
	As becómes his státe	entómb his córpse,
	And withdráw not thysélf	when he breáthes his lást.
17.	Make bítter waíl	and make hót lamént,
	And his moúrning condúct	as fíts his desért—
	A dáy or twó	on accoúnt of teárs;
	Then consóle thysélf	as concérning griéf.

[1] In *v.* 17 a Heb. Text reads המר בני והתם מספד, 'Make bitter (show bitterness), my son, and fulfil lamentation', but LXX πίκρανον κλαυθμὸν καὶ θέρμανον κοπετόν (i.e. בְּכִי for בְּנִי and הָחֵם for הָתֵם) is clearly preferable, and has been adopted above with Smend. In *v.* 17 d Text עָוֹן, 'iniquity', is an error for דָּוֹן; cf. LXX λύπης ἕνεκα.

18. Oút of griéf — comes fórth mischiéf,
So sádness of heárt — prodúces húrt.
20. Túrn not báck — the mínd to him móre,
His mémory dismíss, — and rémember the énd.
21. Remémber him nót, — for he hás no hópe;
Thou prófitest noúght, — and but véxest thysélf.
22. Remémber his fáte, — for 'tis thý fate toó;
Yésterday for hím, — and for theé to-dáy.
23. When résts the deád, — let his mémory rést;
Consóle thysélf — when his lífe depárts.'

Here we observe *hítmārḗr*, *kᵉmíšpāṭṓ*, *wᵉal tíťallḗm* (unless we should stress *wᵉ'ál tíťallḗm*), *hínnāḥḗm* (twice), *míddāwṓn*. It is doubtful, however, whether we can argue from this relatively late specimen of gnomic poetry back to earlier Biblical usage.

§ 6 (*a*). The second stress-accent which would normally fall on the countertone is annulled if the syllable which should receive it, being the first syllable of a word, is in immediate proximity to the stress-accent of the word preceding, without any rhythmical break intervening.

Isa. 33[15]: *hōlḗk ṣᵉdāḳṓt* | *wᵉdōbḗr mēšārī́m*
'He that wálketh jústly | and speáketh upríghtly'.

Here the last word would have borne two stress-accents, *mḗšārī́m*, if it had not been immediately preceded by the stress-accent in *dōbḗr*.

Micah 6[6]: *'iḳḳáph lēlōhē mārṓm*
('Wherewith shall I . . .)
Bow dówn to the Gód of the heíght?'

The counter-stress which *lḗlōhē* might have borne is annulled by the stress on *'iḳḳáph* preceding.

Lam. 3[6]: *bᵉmáḥᵃšakkîm hōšîbánî*

'In glóomy pláces hath He stáblished me'.

Ps. 24[7, 9]: *śᵉʾû šᵉʿārîm rāšēkém*

'Líft up, ye gátes, your heáds'.

In these passages the preceding accent annuls the counter-stress on *hṓšîbánî, rā́šēkém*.

(*b*) The counter-stress which a half-open syllable two places before the stress-accent might bear, is similarly annulled if it would follow immediately after the stress-accent of a word preceding.

Isa. 1[16]: *hāsîrū rṓᵃʿ maʿalᵉlēkém*

'Remóve the évil of your doíngs'.

Isa. 1[21]: *ḳiryā́ neʾᵉmānā́*

'The cíty once-faíthful'.

Isa. 33[16]: *mēmā́w neʾᵉmānîm*

'His wáters unfaíling'.

(*c*) A similar annulment of the retracted accent may take place, when retraction brings it into immediate connexion with a preceding stress-accent.

Isa. 51[7]: *šimʿû ʾēláy yōdᵉʿē ṣédeḳ*
ʿám tōrātî́ bᵉlibbā́m

'Hárk to Me, ye that knów ríghteousness,
Fólk in whose heárt is My láw'.

The third word of the first line, 'knowers of', is normally accented on the ultimate—*yōdᵉʿḗ*. In the full phrase, 'knowers of righteousness', the fact that *ṣédeḳ* 'righteousness' is accented on the first syllable would cause the accent of *yōdᵉʿḗ* to be thrown back on the *ō* preceding—*yṓdᵉʿē ṣédeḳ*, had not the word preceding, *ʾēláy* 'to Me', been accented on the ultimate, thus annulling the stress-accent on the first syllable of *yōdᵉʿē*, which therefore stands rhythmically without any stress. The second stress which *tōrātî́* in the second line might have borne on the *ō* of the first syllable is annulled by the accent of *'ám* preceding.

Ps. 5[4]: *lō 'ḗl ḥāphēṣ réšaʿ 'attā́*

'No Gód willing évil art Thoú'.

The case of *ḥāphēṣ* is just like that of *yōdᵉᵉē* in Isa. 51[7]. An original *ḥāphḗṣ* would have had the accent thrown back upon the open penult to avoid proximity to the accent of *réšaʿ*, but for the fact that this would have brought it into uneuphonic proximity to the accent of *'ḗl*. Thus the word must stand without rhythmical stress.

Isa. 33[14]: *mī́ yāgūr lā́nū* 'Whó of us shall dwéll?' (lit. 'Whó shall-dwell fór-us?'). The accent of *yāgū́r*, which would be thrown back before *lā́nū*, is annulled after *mī́*.

§ 7 (*a*). It seems that in some cases in which a compound term, which would normally take two stresses, is parallel to a simple single-stressed term, the sense of correspondence between the two was powerful enough to cause the former to be allotted one stress only, in order that both might form single 'feet' with corresponding weight, i.e. consuming an equal time in their utterance.

Isa. 1[4]: *ʿāzᵉbū́ 'et Yahwéh*

niʾᵃṣū́ 'et ḳᵉdōš-Yisrāʾḗl

'They have forsáken Yahwéh,

Despísed Israel's-Hóly-One'.

Normally we should stress the second line

niʾᵃṣū́ 'et ḳᵉdṓš Yisrāʾḗl

'Despísed the Hóly-One of Ísrael',

and it is open to take the view that this is here intended; but the fact that the line occurs in the midst of a passage consisting otherwise regularly of two-stressed lines (cf. p. 28) favours the view which is here put forward.

Precisely similar is the opening couplet of the passage from Balaam's oracles quoted on p. 18 as an illustration of Synonymous parallelism. The oracle falls into regular three-stress rhythm.

Num. 23⁷: *min 'Arắm yanḥḗnī Bālā́ḳ*
melek Mō'ā́b mēhā́r^erē ḳédem

'From Arám doth Bálak bríng me,
The-king-of-Moáb from the moúntains of the Eást'.

Clearly *melek Mō'ā́b*, as the equivalent of *Bālā́ḳ*, has precisely similar weight; and to accent *mélek Mō'ā́b* 'The kíng of Moáb' would be to upset the balance.

Another example seems to occur in Micah 6⁷:

ha'ettḗn b^ekōrī́ piš'ī́
p^erī-biṭnī́ ḥaṭṭā́t naphšī́

'Shall I gíve my fírstborn for my faúlt,
Body's-fruít for the sín of my soúl?'

We should normally expect two stresses upon *p^erī́ biṭnī́* 'the fruít of my bódy', but its conversion to a single-stressed term is determined by its parallelism with *b^ekōrī́* 'my fírst-born'.

(*b*) In the following passages—all of them the second members of *Ḳīnā*-verses—we get, apparently, compound expressions taking a single stress.

Lam. 3³⁵: *néged p^enē 'elyṓn*
'Before the-face-of-the-Most-High'.

v. ⁴⁸: *'al šéber bat 'ammī́*
'For the breach of-the-daughter-of-my-people'.

v. ⁶⁶: *mittáḥat š^emē Yahwéh*
'From under the-heavens-of-Yahweh'.

It is noticeable, however, that in each case the preceding word is a Segholate noun, which may have been pronounced as a monosyllable; thus possibly the stressing should be *negd pᵉnḗ*, *'al šebr bát*, *mittaḥt šᵉmḗ*.

Ps. 27[3]: *bᵉzṓt 'ᵃnī bōṭḗᵃḥ*

'For (all) thís would I be tránquil'.

In this second member of a *Ḳīnā*-verse the personal pronoun and participle clearly go together with a single stress-accent.

§ 8. In the stressing or non-stressing of monosyllabic particles considerable freedom appears to have been exercised. The negative *lō* is normally unstressed, as in

Isa. 1[6 b]:

lō zṓrū wᵉlō ḥubbā́šū | *wᵉlọ rukkᵉkā́ baššā́men*

'They are not pressed, and

not bándaged, | and not sóftened with oíntment'.

It may, however, receive a stress if rhythm demands it:

Ps. 5[6]: *lṓ yityaṣṣᵉbū́ hōlᵉlī́m* | *lᵉnéged 'ēnékā*

'Brággarts shall nót take their stánd | in síght of Thine éyes'.

Here, however, it is possible that a stress should fall on the preformative *yit-* of the Hithpa'el form (*lō yítyaṣṣᵉbū́*), as in two cases in the passage cited from Ecclus. 38[16–23] on p. 52.

Similarly, the negative *bal* is stressed in

Ps. 46[6]: *'ᴱlōhī́m bᵉḳirbā́h* | *bál timmṓṭ*

'Gód is in her mídst; | she shall nót be móved'.

The weighty negative *'ēn* 'there is not' (lit. 'nonentity of') is normally stressed, as in

Amos 5[2]: *'ḗn mᵉḳīmā́h*, 'There is nóne to upraíse her'.

But occasionally it may be unstressed:

Ps. 3^3: *rabbī́m 'ōmᵉrī́m lᵉnaphšī́*
'ēn yᵉšū̄'ā́tā lṓ bēlōhī́m
'There are mány that sáy of my soúl,
There is no hélp for hím in Gód'.

The relative *'ᵃšer* may be stressed or unstressed.

Isa. 33^{13}: *šim'ū́ rᵉḥōḳī́m* | *'ᵃšér 'āsī́tī*
'Heár, ye remóte ones, | whát I have dóne'.

Ps. 3^7: *lō 'īrā́ mērī́bᵉbōt 'ā́m*
'ᵃšer sābī́b šā́tū 'ālā́y
'I will not feár for mýriads of fólk,
Which round aboút have sét themselves agaínst me'.

The conjunction *kī* 'if', 'for', &c., though normally without stress (as in Exod. 15^1; Isa. 1^{12}, 51^8; Ps. $3^{6,8}$, &c.), may occasionally receive a stress-accent. So probably in Gen. 4^{24} *kī́ šib'ātáyim yuḳḳam Ḳáyin* (as stressed, 'Íf sevenfóld avenged Caín'); cf. p. 47, and possibly Ps. 27^5 (cf. p. 51) *kī́ yiṣpᵉnḗnī bᵉsukkṓ*.

Prepositions are normally unstressed (except in suffix-forms), but there may be exceptions. Thus, it is probable that *'im* 'with' receives a stress in Micah 6^8 *wᵉhaṣnēᵃ' léket 'ím 'ᴱlōhékā* (as stressed, 'And humbly wálking wíth thy Gód').

The juxtaposition of two particles enhances the probability that one of them will be stressed. So *gam kī* 'yea, though' in

Lam. 3^8: *gám kī 'ez'áḳ wa'ᵃšāwwḗᵃ'*
'Yeá, though I cáll and cry oút'.

Isa. 1^{15}: *gám kī tarbū́ tᵉphillā́*
'Yeá, though ye múltiply práyer'.

It is not, however, necessary that one of two conjoined particles should receive a stress-accent. Cf. unstressed *kī 'im* 'but', in

Micah 6^8: *kī 'im 'ᵃsṓt mišpā́t wᵉ'áhᵃbat ḥésed*
'But dóing of jústice and lóving of kíndness'.

APPENDED NOTE.

Rabbi Azariah di Rossi (A.D. 1514–88) of Ferrara, published in 1574 a work entitled *Me'ōr 'Ēnayim* ('Light of the Eyes') in which he put forward a theory of Hebrew rhythm which is clearly on the right lines, anticipating as it does in main essentials the view which is commonly held at the present day, and which we have illustrated in the foregoing discussion. According to Azariah, 'there can be no doubt that the sacred songs possess measures and proportions (מדות וערכים); these, however, are not dependent upon the number of syllables, whether full or half syllables, according to the system of versification which is now in use among us', and which is based on the Arabic model; 'but their proportions and measures are *by the number of Things and their Parts* (במספר הענינים וחלקיהם), i.e. Subject and Predicate and their adjuncts (מנושא ונשוא והמתחבר אליהם) in each written phrase and proposition. Thus, a phrase may consist of two measures,[1] and with the second phrase which is attached to it these become four; or, again, it may contain three measures, and with the second phrase which corresponds they become six complete measures. Here is an example. *Yᵉmīnᵉkā 'ᵃdōnāy* (Exod. 15^6) "Thy-right-hand, O-Lord" is one phrase by itself consisting of two parts; *ne'dārī bakkōᵃḥ* "is-glorious in-strength" is its equivalent attached to it, and together they make four (a tetrameter). So, again, *yᵉmīnᵉkā 'ᵃdōnāy* "Thy-right-hand, O-Lord", repeated, gives two more; *tir'aṣ 'ōyēb* "doth-shatter the-foe", a further two, making four. And in like manner—

[1] מדות, 'measures', clearly has the force of 'rhythmical stresses'.

'āmár 'ōyēb	*'erdōph 'assīg*
'ᵃḥallēḳ šālál	*timlā'ēmō naphšī*
'āriḳ ḥarbī	*tōrīšēmō yādī*
nāšáphtā bᵉrūḥᵃkā	*kissāmō yām*
"The-énemy saíd,	I-will-pursué, I-will-over-táke;
I-will-divíde the-spoíl,	my-lúst shall-be-sáted-on-them;
I-will-dráw my-swórd,	my-hánd shall-destróy-them.
Thou-didst-blów with-Thy-wínd,	the-seá cóvered-them".

The song *Ha'ᵃzīnū*, "Give ear" (Deut. 32), however, consists of three + three measures, which make six (hexameters). Thus—

ha'ᵃzīnū haššāmáyim wa'ᵃdabbērā	*wᵉtišmá' hā'áreṣ 'imrē-phī*
yā'ᵃrōph kammāṭár liḳḥī	*tizzál kaṭṭál 'imrātī*
"Give-eár, O-heávens, and-I-will-speák;	and-let-heár the-eárth my-mouth's-wórds:
Let-dróp, like-the-raín, my-advíce;	let-distíll, like-the-déw, my-discoúrse."'

Proceeding to remark that one poem may exhibit two different forms of rhythm, e.g. 2 + 2 combined with 3 + 3 measure, Azariah illustrates this from Exod. 15, the Song of the Well (Num. 21[17f.]), and the Prayer of Habakkuk (Hab. 3). After showing that the main part of this last poem is in 3 + 3 measure, he goes on to deal with *v.*[17] as exhibiting, on his view, 2 + 2 measure. 'But the verse *kī tᵉ'ēnā lō tiphraḥ*, "Though the fig-tree shall not blossom", observes another method, Subject and Predicate—*kī-tᵉ'ēnā* Subject; *lō-tiphraḥ* Predicate; and so with the whole verse, which embraces twelve terms resolving themselves into six separate statements.[1] For you should not reckon either the syllables or the words; *but only the Things* (רק הענינים). And for this reason a small word is very often attached to the word that is next to it.' [2]

A fuller account of Azariah's argument may be found in Lowth, *op. cit.*, pp. xli ff. It will be seen, from so much as we have quoted, that his theory fits in, in the main, with the rhythmical rules which we have attempted to frame; though he had not arrived at the conception of a single word bearing two rhythmical stresses, which we have formulated under § 5. 'I am aware', he says, 'that there are many verses which I cannot accommodate to the rules which I have given;

[1] וכן כל הפסוק שהוא כולל י"ב דבורים אשר ישובו לששת מאמרים פוסקים. Lowth, in his excellent reproduction of Azariah's argument in the Introduction to his *Book of Isaiah*, pp. xli ff., misunderstands this statement when he renders it (p. xlv), 'So in a verse containing twelve terms, those terms may be reduced to six measures'. The reference is not to any hypothetical verse which might contain such a number, but to Hab. 3^{17}, about which the writer is talking. The twelve expressions or terms making six distinct statements are as follows:

kī-t^{e}'ēnā́ lō-tiphrā́ḥ	*w^{e}'ēn-y^{e}bū́l bagg^{e}phānī́m*
kiḥḥḗš ma'^{a}sē-záyit	*ūš^{e}dēmṓt lō-'āsā-'ṓkel*
gāzár mimmiklā-ṣṓn	*w^{e}'ēn-bāḳā́r bār^{e}phātī́m*

'Though-the-fíg-tree shall-not-blóssom,	neither-fruít be-in-the-vínes,
Shall-have-faíled the-olive's-próduce,	and-the-fiélds not-yielded-food,
He-shall-have-cút-off flock-from-fóld,	and-no-hérd be-in-the-stàlls.'

Here we have, in each separate statement, the two parts (Subject and Predicate) to which Azariah is referring, except in *gāzar mimmiklā ṣōn*, where the indefinite Subject is included in the verb, and the proposition seems to consist of three parts. Apart from this difficulty, Azariah's conclusion can be defended; though a case could also be made out for regarding the verse as consisting of 3 + 3 stress rhythm.

[2] נרחקת לאשר אצלה, rendered 'is attached to the word that is next to it', seems properly to mean 'loses its stress to that which is next to it'.

and perhaps the unexplained may be more numerous than the explicable. Yet by aid of this discussion scholars may receive new light, and be able to discover that which has escaped me.' The reason why we have quoted this far-sighted Rabbi is for the emphasis which he lays on *Things and their Parts*, as determining rhythm (cf. the passages italicized above), i. e. upon the sense-connexion as affecting the rhythmical balance. While accepting the rhythmical rules which we have formulated, we may hold that there probably exist cases in which sense-connexion and balance override other rules; and this in fact is a conclusion after which we were feeling in § 7 when we explained *ḳᵉdōš Yisrā'ēl* as bearing a single stress-accent on account of its balance with *Yahwéh*, and *melek Mō'ā́b* in the same way as balancing *Bālā́ḳ* in the parallel stichos. These considerations may help us in regard to passages which cannot otherwise be reduced to rule.

II

THE USE OF PARALLELISM BY OUR LORD

Synonymous Parallelism.

THE use of Synonymous Parallelism by our Lord is confined, for the most part, to single couplets, or (as most often in O.T.) to couplets combined with Synthetic or Antithetic couplets. The most striking example of the continuous use of this form of parallelism comes from M, the reply to the petition of the two sons of Zebedee, where we have four Synonymous couplets combined with one (the third) Antithetic and one (the sixth) Synthetic.

Mark $10^{38\ ff.}$ = Matt. $20^{22\ ff.}$.

'Ye know not what ye ask.
Can ye drink of the cup which I drink?
Or be baptized with the baptism wherewith I am baptized?

. . . .

The cup which I drink shall ye drink,
And with the baptism wherewith I am baptized shall ye be baptized.
But to sit on My right hand and on My left is not Mine to give,
But for those for whom it is prepared of My Father.

. . . .

Ye know that

The princes of the nations exercise lordship over them,
And the magnates exercise authority over them.[1]

But it shall not be so among you; but

He that would be great among you, let him be your minister,
And he that would be first among you, let him be your slave.[2]

Like as the Son of man came not to be ministered unto, but to minister,
And to give His life a ransom for many.'

Instances of synonymous distichs or tristichs occurring singly or in groups of two or three are frequent. We have the following from M:

Mark 3^4 = Luke 6^9.

'Is it lawful on the sabbath to do good or to do harm?
To save a life or to kill?'[3]

Mark $3^{24, 25}$ = Matt. 12^{25} = Luke 11^{17}.

'Every kingdom divided against itself is desolated,
And house against house falleth.'[4]

[1] Cf. Luke 22^{25}.

[2] Cf. Luke 22^{26}.

[3] Luke ἀπολέσαι in place of ἀποκτεῖναι. Matt. $12^{11, 12}$ omits this saying, and gives in place of it the comparison of the sheep fallen into a pit.

[4] Luke's text given above is most compact, and in the character of synonymous parallelism. Matt.'s second stichos runs:

'And every city or house divided against itself shall not stand'.

In Mark we read:

'And if a kingdom be divided against itself,
That kingdom cannot stand.
And if a house be divided against itself,
That house cannot stand.'

The meaning of the second stichos in Luke is open to question.

Mark $3^{28, 29}$.

'All sins shall be forgiven to the sons of men,
And the blasphemies wherewith soever they shall blaspheme:
But he that blasphemeth against the Holy Spirit hath never forgiveness,
But is guilty of an eternal sin.'[1]

Mark 4^{22} = Luke 8^{17}.

'There is nothing hid that shall not be made manifest,
Nor secret that shall not come to light.'[2]

Mark 4^{30} = Luke 13^{18}.

'How shall we liken the kingdom of God?
Or in what parable shall we set it forth?'[3]

Mark $8^{17, 18}$.

'Do ye not perceive, nor understand?
Have ye your heart hardened?

Vulg. 'domus supra domum cadet' takes the statement as an enlargement of *ἐρημοῦται* in stichos 1, and this is adopted by Plummer, who renders 'house falleth on house', with the alternative 'house after house falleth'. The original Aramaic, which may be assumed to have been וּבַיְתָא עַל־בַּיְתָא נָפֵל, is as ambiguous as the Greek; but the interpretation of the saying given by Matt. and Mark is the more probable.

[1] The parallel passage in Matt. $12^{31, 32}$ casts the saying into antithetical couplets. No parallel in Luke.

[2] On Mark's *ἐὰν μὴ ἵνα . . . ἀλλ' ἵνα* as a mistranslation of the Aramaic *dᵉ* relative (rightly rendered in Luke), cf. the writer's *Aramaic Origin of the Fourth Gospel*, p. 76. This saying occurs again in Q in a different context in Matt. 10^{26} = Luke 12^{2}.

[3] Luke: 'Unto what is the kingdom of God like?
And whereunto shall I liken it?'

Matt. $13^{31 \text{ ff.}}$ gives the parable of the mustard seed without this introduction.

Having eyes, see ye not?
And having ears, hear ye not?
And do ye not remember?'[1]

Mark 8^{34} = Matt. 16^{24} = Luke 9^{23}.

'If any wisheth to come after Me, let him deny himself,
And let him take up his cross, and follow Me.'[2]

Mark 9^{19} = Matt. 17^{17} = Luke 9^{41}.

'O faithless generation!
How long shall I be with you?
How long shall I suffer you?'[3]

Mark 10^{14} = Matt. 19^{14} = Luke 18^{16}.

'Suffer the little children,
And forbid them not to come unto Me.'[4]

Mark 13^{8} = Matt. 24^{7} = Luke 21^{10}.

'Nation shall rise against nation,
And kingdom against kingdom.'

Mark $13^{24, 25}$ = Matt. 24^{29}.

'The sun shall be darkened,
And the moon shall not give her light,
And the stars shall fall from heaven,
And the powers of the heavens shall be shaken.'[5]

[1] This is reduced in Matt. 16^{9} to the opening and closing words οὔπω νοεῖτε, οὐδὲ μνημονεύετε . . .

[2] Luke adds καθ' ἡμέραν after τὸν σταυρὸν αὐτοῦ, and there are rhythmical reasons for considering this original. Cf. p. 142, foot-note.

[3] Matt. and Luke add καὶ διεστραμμένη after ἄπιστος. Luke destroys the synonymous parallelism by substituting καί for the second ἕως πότε, so that the two clauses read as one.

[4] Following the order of Matt. Mark and Luke connect ἄφετε with ἔρχεσθαι (ἐλθεῖν), but the parallelism is better if we take it absolutely in the sense 'let them alone', 'do not interfere with them'. Cf. Luke 13^{8}: ἄφες αὐτὴν καὶ τοῦτο τὸ ἔτος.

[5] Luke $21^{25, 26}$ offers a paraphrase which destroys parallelism and rhythm.

In Q, as is natural, Synonymous and other forms of parallelism are frequent. The following are examples of Synonymous parallelism:

Luke $6^{27, 28}$ = Matt. 5^{44}.

'Love your enemies,
Do good to your haters,
Bless your cursers,
Pray for your persecutors.'[1]

Matt. 5^{45}.

'He causeth His sun to rise upon evil and good,
And raineth upon just and unjust.'[2]

Luke $12^{22, 23}$ = Matt. 6^{25}.

'Be not anxious for your life, what ye shall eat,
Neither for your body, what ye shall put on:
Is not the life more than meat?
And the body than raiment?'[3]

Matt. $7^{7, 8}$ = Luke $11^{9, 10}$.

'Ask, and it shall be given you;
Seek, and ye shall find;
Knock, and it shall be opened to you.
For every asker receiveth;
And the seeker findeth;
And to the knocker it shall be opened.'

Matt. $10^{24, 25}$ = Luke 6^{40}.

'The disciple is not above his master,
Nor the servant above his lord.

[1] Matt. has only the first and last stichoi, with διωκόντων in place of Luke's ἐπηρεαζόντων.

[2] Luke $6^{35\,b}$ seems to be the equivalent—'For He is kind toward the unthankful and evil'.

[3] Matt. adds 'or what ye shall drink' at the end of stichos 1. This destroys the balance of the couplet.

Enough for the disciple that he be as his master,
And the servant as his lord.'[1]

Matt. 11^{12} = Luke 16^{16}.

'The kingdom of heaven suffereth violence,
And the violent take it by force.'[2]

Matt. 12^{30} = Luke 11^{23}.

'He that is not with Me is against Me,
And he that gathereth not with Me scattereth.'

Matt. 23^{29} = Luke 11^{47}.

'Ye build the sepulchres of the prophets,
And adorn the tombs of the righteous.'[3]

Matt. $24^{50, 51}$ = Luke 12^{46}.

'The lord of that servant shall come in a day when he expecteth not,
And in an hour when he knoweth not,

And shall cut him asunder,
And appoint him his portion with the hypocrites.

There shall be weeping
And gnashing of teeth.'[4]

The following examples—though presumably from Q—are found in Matt. only:

Matt. 7^{6}.

'Give not that which is holy to the dogs,
Neither cast ye your pearls before swine,

[1] Luke omits the parallel stichos in each couplet.

[2] Luke reads: 'The kingdom of heaven is preached,
And every man entereth violently into it.'
This is inferior to Matt.

[3] Luke has: 'Ye build the tombs of the prophets,
But your fathers killed them.'
Here the second stichos summarizes *vv.* $^{30, 31}$ of Matt.

[4] The last couplet is found in Matt. only in this connexion. Cf. Matt. 8^{12}, $13^{42, 50}$, 22^{13}, 25^{30}, Luke 13^{28}.

Lest they trample them under their feet,
And turn again and rend you.'

Matt. 10^{41}.

'He that receiveth a prophet in the name of a prophet
Shall receive a prophet's reward,
And he that receiveth a righteous man in the name of a righteous man
Shall receive a righteous man's reward.'

The following occur in Luke only:

Luke 12^{48}.

'To whomsoever much is given,
Of him shall much be required;
And to whom they commit much,
Of him will they ask the more.'

Luke 15^{32}.

'This thy brother was dead and is alive,
He was lost and is found.'

Luke $19^{43, 44}$.

'Thine enemies shall cast a bank about thee,
And shall compass thee and keep thee in on every side,
And shall lay thee even with the ground, and thy children within thee,
And shall not leave in thee one stone upon another.'[1]

[1] Some would interpret ἐδαφιοῦσίν σε 'shall dash thee to the ground' (so R.V.). Cf. Plummer's note *ad loc.*, where the argument that A.V.'s rendering, 'lay thee even with the ground', makes the clause 'tautological' with the following clause, has no weight against this interpretation, but rather the reverse.

Luke 24^{38}.

'Why are ye troubled?
And why do reasonings arise in your hearts?
See My hands and My feet that it is I Myself;
Handle Me and see.'

The following instances of Synonymous parallelism are gathered from the Fourth Gospel:

John 3^{11}.

'That which we know we speak,
And that which we have seen we testify.'

John 4^{36}.

'He that reapeth receiveth wages,
And gathereth fruit unto life eternal.'

John 6^{35}.

'He that cometh to Me shall never hunger,
And he that believeth on Me shall never thirst.'

John 6^{55}.

'My flesh is meat indeed,
And My blood is drink indeed.'

John 7^{34}.

'Ye shall seek Me, and shall not find Me,
And where I am ye cannot come.'

John 7^{37}.

'If any man thirst, let him come unto Me;
And let him drink that believeth on Me.'[1]

John 12^{26}.

'If any man serve Me, let him follow Me;
And where I am, there shall My servant be.'

[1] On this passage cf. the present writer's *Aramaic Origin of the Fourth Gospel*, p. 109 f. The connexion of ὁ πιστεύων εἰς ἐμέ with καὶ πινέτω preceding, and not with the following clause, was made by the most ancient western interpreters.

John 12^{31}.

'Now is the judgment of this world;
Now shall the prince of this world be cast out.'

John 13^{16}.

'The servant is not greater than his lord,
Nor is the messenger greater than him that sent him.'

John 14^{27}.

'Peace I leave with you,
My peace I give unto you.
. . . . . .
Let not your heart be troubled,
Neither let it be afraid.'

John 15^{26}.

'The Comforter, Whom I will send you from the Father,
The Spirit of truth, Who proceedeth from the Father.'

John 20^{17}.

'I ascend unto My Father and your Father,
And unto My God and your God.'

John 20^{27}.

'Reach hither thy finger, and behold My hands;
And reach hither thy hand, and thrust it into My side.'

Antithetic Parallelism.

Our Lord's teaching, like the gnomic teaching of the O.T. authors of the Wisdom-literature, tended to express itself in sharply marked antitheses; and these antitheses are commonly expressed in balancing couplets. The antithesis is very often produced by the use of opposites, e.g.:

Matt. 7^{17}.

'Every good tree bringeth forth good fruits,
But the corrupt tree bringeth forth evil fruits.'

John 3^{6}.

'That which is born of the flesh is flesh,
And that which is born of the spirit is spirit.'

Occasionally, though somewhat rarely, it takes the form of contrast between positive and negative in identical terms. Thus:

Matt. $6^{14,15}$.

'If ye forgive men their trespasses,
Your heavenly Father also shall forgive you;
But if ye forgive not men their trespasses,
Neither shall your Father forgive your trespasses.'

John 3^{18}.

'He that believeth on Him is not condemned;
He that believeth not is already condemned.'

Very frequently these two forms are combined, and we have an antithesis by contrast between opposites as well as by that between positive and negative. Examples are:

Matt. 15^{11}.

'Not that which goeth into the mouth defileth the man,
But that which cometh out of the mouth, that defileth
the man.'

John 8^{35}.

'The slave abideth not in the house for ever;
The son abideth for ever.'

A very striking form of antithesis is one in which the contrast is obtained by simple inversion of terms in the parallel clauses. Of this nature are:

Matt. 10^{39}.

'He that findeth his life shall lose it;
And he that loseth his life for My sake shall find it.'

Matt. 20^{16}.

'So the last shall be first,
And the first last.'

Matt. 23^{12}.

'Whosoever exalteth himself shall be humbled;
And whosoever humbleth himself shall be exalted.'

John 9^{39}.

'For judgment came I into this world,
That they which see not may see,
And that they which see may become blind.'

Similar in construction is:

Mark 2^{27}.

'The sabbath was made for man,
And not man for the sabbath.'

In order now to illustrate the widespread and significant character of this form of parallelism in our Lord's teaching, we will take, as far as possible, all the most striking instances of antithesis throughout the four Gospels and group them according to their sources. We shall not cite the sayings in full, but merely set the antithetical elements in them the one against the other, in order clearly to bring out the form of construction.

The following instances have been collected from M:

Matt. 12^{32} = Mark $3^{28, 29}$.

Against the Son of man	forgiven
Against the Holy Spirit	not forgiven [1]

Mark 4^{25} = Matt. 13^{12}.

Having	increased
Not having	diminished [2]

Mark 7^{8}.

Forsaking	the commandment	of God
Holding	the tradition	of men [3]

Mark 7^{9}.

Annulling	the commandment	of God
Keeping	the tradition	of yours [3]

Mark 7^{15} = Matt. 15^{11}.

Going into mouth	not defiling
Coming out of mouth	defiling

Mark 8^{35} = Matt. 16^{25} = Luke 9^{24}.

Saving his life	losing it
Losing his life	saving it [4]

[1] The antithesis is given in the form in which it occurs in Matt. Mark gives two synonymously parallel couplets, which have already been cited on p. 65.

[2] The saying stands in different contexts in the two Gospels.

[3] Omitted in the parallel narrative of Matt. 15^{1-20}.

[4] This runs in Matt. and Luke—

'Whosoever willeth to save his life, shall lose it;
But whosoever shall lose his life for My sake, shall find (save) it.'

Mark adds, 'and the gospel's' after 'for My sake', which clearly overweights the clause. As, then, it is improbable that both Matt. and Luke should have improved upon the form of Mark's parallelism by excision of the words καὶ τοῦ εὐαγγελίου, we must infer that they depended upon a source of information superior to Mark, i.e. probably Q; in other words, the passage is an indication that Mark knew and

Mark 10^{9} = Matt. 19^{6}.

God | joined together
Man | put asunder

Mark 10^{27} = Matt. 19^{26} = Luke 18^{27}.

Man | impossible
God | possible[1]

Mark 10^{31} = Matt. 19^{30} (20^{16}).

First | last
Last | first

Mark 13^{31} = Matt. 24^{35} = Luke 21^{33}.

Heaven and earth | shall pass away
My words | shall not pass away

Mark 14^{38} = Matt. 26^{41}.

Spirit | zealous
Flesh | weak

used Q, and in this case has glossed it to the detriment of the parallelistic form of the antithesis. A similar statement, apparently from Q, is noted on p. 142.

[1] This example offers another instance in which Mark is clearly inferior to the other Synoptists. The typical form of antithesis (as witnessed by numerous other examples) is that given by Matt.:

'With man this is impossible,
But with God all things are possible.'

This has been somewhat paraphrased by Luke:

'The things which are impossible with men
Are possible with God',

a form in which the strict parallelism of the two antithetical statements is modified so as to produce a *single* statement—still, nothing is added.

In Mark, however, we read:

'With men it is impossible,
But not with God;
For all things are possible with God.'

Here the insertion of 'But not with God', which is really redundant by the side of the following line, has the effect of marring the sharpness and balance of the antithesis. Clearly the addition is a gloss.

Mark 14^{7} = Matt. 26^{11} = John 12^{8}.

The poor	ye have always with you
Me	ye have not always with you.[1]

The following instances come from Q:

Matt. $6^{19, 20}$ = Luke 12^{33}.

Treasures on earth	moth, rust, thieves
Treasures in heaven	no moth, rust, thieves[2]

Matt. $6^{22, 23}$ = Luke 11^{34}.

Single eye	light
Evil eye	dark

Matt. $7^{13, 14}$ = Luke 13^{24}.

Broad gate	destruction	many enterers
Narrow gate	life	few finders[3]

Matt. 7^{17} (12^{33}) = Luke 6^{43}.

Good tree	good fruit
Bad tree	bad fruit

Matt. $10^{32, 33}$ = Luke 12^{8}.

Confessor	confessed
Denier	denied[4]

[1] Again we find that the sharp and telling antithesis of Matt. and John,

'The poor ye have always with you;
(But) Me ye have not always',

is destroyed in Mark by the insertion after the first stichos of the words, 'And whenever ye will ye can do (them) good'. This must be thought to be a gloss adding a correct, but unnecessary, explanation of the implication of the first clause.

[2] Luke has nothing corresponding to stichos 1, and therefore gives no antithesis. The injunction as given by him, however, comes in a context which falls into a form of rhythm for the use of which by our Lord there is strong evidence elsewhere. Cf. p. 87.

[3] Luke gives the injunction in a form which destroys the antithesis; but here again the passage and its context seem to be marked by a form of rhythm. Cf. p. 87.

[4] Matt.: 'I will confess . . . will deny'; Luke: 'The Son of man shall confess . . . he shall be denied.'

Matt. 11²³ = Luke 10¹⁵.

Exalted | to heaven
Descending | to hades

Matt. 11²⁵ = Luke 10²¹.

Concealed | wise
Revealed | babes

Matt. 12³⁵ = Luke 6⁴⁵.

Good man | good treasure | good things
Bad man | bad treasure | bad things

Matt. 10³⁹ (= Luke 17³³).

Finding his life | losing it
Losing his life | finding it [1]

Matt. 23¹² = Luke 14¹¹ (18¹⁴).

Exalting himself | humbled
Humbling himself | exalted.

The following examples in Matthew—apparently from Q—have no parallel in Luke:

Matt. 5¹⁹.

Looses | least in kingdom
Performs | great in kingdom

Matt. 6¹⁴, ¹⁵.

If ye forgive | your heavenly Father shall forgive you
If ye forgive not | your heavenly Father shall not forgive you

Matt. 7¹⁵.

Outwardly | sheep
Inwardly | wolves

[1] The Luke passage (which occurs in a different context) takes the form:
Seeking to preserve his life | losing it
Losing | preserving it alive.
Cf. the similar statement from M noticed on p. 85.

Matt. 16^{19}, 18^{18}.

Bound on earth	bound in heaven
Loosed on earth	loosed in heaven

Matt. 22^{14}.

Many	called
Few	chosen[1]

Matt. 23^{27}.

Without	beautiful
Within	full of corruption

Matt. 23^{28}.

Without	righteous
Within	full of hypocrisy, &c.

The following occur in Luke only:

Luke $12^{47,48}$.

Knowing his lord's will	beaten with many stripes
Not knowing	beaten with few stripes

Luke 16^{10}.

Faithful in a very little	faithful in much
Dishonest in a very little	dishonest in much[2]

Luke 16^{15}.

Exalted	among men
Abomination	before God

Luke 16^{25}.

Dives	good things
Lazarus	evil things
Lazarus	comforted
Dives	tormented

[1] At the end of the parable of the wedding-feast. The saying is not found after Luke's version of this parable, 14^{16-24}.

[2] Cf. Matt. $25^{21, 23}$

Luke 17^{3}.

If he sin	rebuke him
If he repent	forgive him[1]

Luke 23^{28}.

Weep not	for Me
Weep	for yourselves.

Turning to the Fourth Gospel, we find that Antithetic parallelism is remarkably frequent, and that it takes the same form as in the Synoptists. The following are examples:

John 3^{6}.

Flesh-born	flesh
Spirit-born	spirit

John 3^{18}.

Believing	not condemned
Not believing	already condemned

John $3^{20,21}$.

Evil-doer	hates light	condemnation
Truth-doer	comes to light	justification

John 3^{31}.

He from above	above all
He from the earth	of the earth

John 3^{36}.

Believing	has life
Disbelieving	shall not see life

John $4^{13,14}$.

Earthly water	thirst again
Spiritual water	thirst no more

John 4^{22}.

Ye worship	that ye know not
We worship	that we know

[1] Cf. Matt. $18^{15, 21, 22}$.

John 5^{29}.

Good-doers	life
Evil-doers	judgment

John 5^{43}.

I	My Father's name	rejection
Another	his own name	reception

John 6^{27}.

Labour not	for perishing bread
(Labour)	for everlasting bread

John 6^{32}.

Moses	gave you not	the bread from heaven
My Father	giveth you	the true bread from heaven

John 7^{6}.

My time	not yet present
Your time	always ready

John 8^{23}.

Ye	from beneath	of this world
I	from above	not of this world

John 8^{35}.

Slave	not abiding
Son	abiding

John 9^{39}.

That those not seeing	may see
That those seeing	may become blind

John 9^{41}.

Blind	no sin
Seeing	sin

John 10^{10}.

The thief	comes to slay, &c.
I	come to give life

John $11^{9,10}$.

Walking in the day | not stumbling | light
Walking in the night | stumbling | no light

John 12^{8}.

The poor | ye have always with you
Me | ye have not always [1]

John 12^{24}.

Seed not dying | sterile
Seed dying | fertile

John 12^{25}.

Loving life | losing it
Hating life | keeping it [2]

John 14^{19}.

The world | seeth Me no more
Ye | see Me

John 15^{2}.

Not bearing fruit | removal
Bearing fruit | tending

John 15^{15}.

Slaves | ignorant
Friends | informed

John 16^{33}.

In Me | peace
In the world | tribulation.

[1] Cf. the occurrence of this saying in M, p. 76, with foot-note.
[2] Cf. the similar sayings in M and Q, pp. 74, 141–2, with foot-note.

A special form of Antithetic parallelism is one which involves an argument *a minori ad maius*. This form of argument is included among the seven rules of logic formulated by the great Rabbi Hillel, who flourished just before the Christian era. He called it *ḳal wā-ḥômer*, i.e. 'light and heavy' = from the less to the greater. We find the following examples of this among our Lord's sayings. From Q:

Matt. 7^{3-5} = Luke $6^{41,42}$.

'Why beholdest thou the mote that is in thy brother's eye,
But regardest not the beam that is in thine own eye?
Or how canst thou say to thy brother,
"Let me cast out the mote that is in thine eye",
And, lo, the beam is in thine own eye.
Hypocrite!
Cast out first the beam out of thine own eye,
And then shalt thou see clearly to cast out the mote out of thy brother's eye!'[1]

Matt. 7^{11} = Luke 11^{13}.

'If ye, being evil, know how to give good gifts to your children,
How much more shall your heavenly Father give good things to them that ask Him?'[2]

[1] A similar saying is ascribed to Rabbi Tarphon (*c.* A.D. 100) in the Talmudic treatise *'Arākhîn*:—'If one says, "Take the mote (קיסם) out of thine eyes", he replies, "Take the beam (קורה) out of thine eyes".' Cf. Buxtorf, *Lex.* s. v. קיסם; Wünsche, *Neue Beiträge zur Erläuterung der Evangelien*, p. 100. Parallel occurrences are given by Strack and Billerbeck, *Das Evang. nach Matt.*, *ad loc.*

[2] In stichos 2, Luke, in place of 'good things' of Matt., has 'the Holy Spirit'. This must be regarded as an interpretation of the meaning of ἀγαθά.

From Matt. alone (Q ?):

Matt. 10^{25b}.

'If they have called the master of the house Beelzebul,
How much more those of his household?'

From Luke alone:

Luke $16^{11,12}$.

'If then ye have not been trusty in the unrighteous mammon,
Who will entrust to you the true?
And if ye have not been trusty in that which is another's,
Who will give you that which is your own?'

Luke 23^{31}.

'If they do these things in a green tree,
What shall be done in the dry?'

From the Fourth Gospel:

John 3^{12}.

'If I told you of earthly things, and ye believed not,
How shall ye believe if I tell you of heavenly things?'

John 5^{47}.

'If ye believe not his writings,
How shall ye believe My words?'

We may now observe that, through this simple classification and tabulation of our Lord's use of Antithetic parallelism throughout the Gospels, we seem to have reached results of remarkable interest and importance.

In the first place, we find that this form of parallelism characterizes our Lord's teaching in all the Gospel-sources. We have it in M and Q frequently, in the matter peculiar to Luke, and, most markedly of all, in the Fourth Gospel. This is conclusive evidence that our Lord did so frame His teaching; and it is obvious that a maxim cast in Antithetic parallelism would fix itself in men's minds more readily and surely than if it were framed in any other form. No one could hear such a saying as

'He that findeth his life shall lose it;
And he that loseth his life for My sake shall find it',

and subsequently forget precisely how the Speaker had expressed Himself. In this and in similar forms of antithesis we may surely believe that we possess our Lord's *ipsissima verba* more nearly than in any sentence otherwise expressed.

Secondly, the phenomenon has an important bearing upon the authenticity of the discourses in the Fourth Gospel. The unlikeness of these discourses to the comparatively simple teaching recorded by the Synoptists has been the subject of much comment, and has been used as an argument against their authenticity. To the present writer the difference of audience—in the Synoptists for the most part simple Galilaean peasants; in the Fourth Gospel usually Rabbinic disputants at Jerusalem—offers a sufficient explanation of the difference in form;[1] yet we might, if the Johannine discourses are substantially genuine, expect to find some characteristic turn of expression making a bond of connexion between the simple teaching and the more abstruse. In this use of Antithetic parallelism we have it. Yet, frequent and characteristic as this form of speech is in the Johannine discourses, it is clearly no artificial *imitation* of the style of the Synoptic

[1] Cf. the writer's *Aramaic Origin of the Fourth Gospel*, p. 143.

teaching. The antitheses of John are no servile reproduction of those of the Synoptists. They are not dragged in to produce an appearance of resemblance to the Synoptic discourses, but are an integral part of the teaching in which they occur.

Thirdly, as regards the Marcan source in relation to its parallels in the other Synoptists, we have gleaned a few clear indications that blind confidence in Mark, as necessarily preserving the most original form of sayings that are supposed to be derived from him, is wrong. In three cases, viz. Mark 8^{35} = Matt. 16^{25} = Luke 9^{24}; Mark 10^{27} = Matt. 19^{26} = Luke 18^{27}; Mark 14^{7} = Matt. 26^{11} = John 12^{8} (pp. 74–6), we conclude, on the evidence of similarly formed antitheses, that Mark has glossed his original, and that this original is more nearly preserved in one or more of the parallel sources. Let us cite the three Marcan passages, italicizing the words which are not found in the other sources.

Mark 8^{35}.

'For whosoever would save his life shall lose it;
And whosoever shall lose his life for My sake *and the gospel's* shall save it.'[1]

Mark 10^{27f}.

'With men it is impossible,
But not with God;
For all things are possible with God.'

[1] In Luke 17^{33} the antithesis takes the form:

'Whosoever shall seek to gain his life shall lose it;
But whosoever shall lose (it) shall preserve it.'

This, though probably somewhat paraphrastic as compared with the other versions, may be correct in omitting 'for My sake' as well as 'and the gospel's', the original antithesis running:

man d^{e}maḥḥē naphšēh mawbēd lāh
ūman d^{e}mawbēd naphšēh maḥḥē lāh.

Mark 14^7.

'For ye have the poor always with you,
And whensoever ye will ye can do them good:
But Me ye have not always.'

Removing the italicized words in each of these passages, we have the antitheses as they appear, in the first case in Matthew and Luke, in the second in Matthew, in the third in Matthew and John; *and* we restore the sharp-pointed form of antithesis to which numerous other examples witness as characteristic of our Lord's teaching, and which, in the cases in question, has been in some degree destroyed by the additional words found in Mark. It may readily be admitted that, if these three Marcan passages stood alone, without parallels in the other Gospels, we should not be justified in ruling out the italicized words as unoriginal merely in order to bring the antithesis into line with the form of other different antitheses, since it is obvious that our Lord was not necessarily tied down to one hard-and-fast form of antithetical expression. But, inasmuch as we *do* find parallels in the other Gospels in which the sayings are given in conformity with the normal type, it may be emphatically maintained that these parallels are vastly more likely to represent our Lord's *ipsissima verba* than are the Marcan forms; since the alternative explanation, viz. that the authors of the other Gospels, noticing a variation from the normal type in Mark, have deliberately omitted some of his words in order to conform with that type, can hardly be contemplated seriously.

We conclude, then, that here is a piece of important evidence that in the sections of Matthew and Luke which are parallel with Mark, these former Synoptists were not always dependent upon Mark only, but had access to a source which was in some respects more original. And since the cases in point are records of *teaching*, and Q seems to have formed mainly a corpus of our Lord's teaching, we may assume that this source was Q. Probably, then, Mark also knew Q, and to some extent employed it and, in the passages in question, glossed its contents.

Fourthly, if the question be raised whether Matthew or Luke has preserved the more original form of Q, it will be found by reference to the foot-notes given under the examples of *Antithetic parallelism*, Matt. 19^{26} = Luke 18^{27}; Matt. 6^{19,20} = Luke 12^{33}; Matt. 7^{13,14} = Luke 13^{24} (pp. 75, 76), and under the head of *Synonymous parallelism*, Matt. 5^{45} = Luke 6^{35b}; Matt. 10^{24,25} = Luke 6^{40}; Matt. 11^{12} = Luke 16^{16}; Matt. 23^{29} = Luke 11^{47} (pp. 67 ff.), to which we may add the examples from M, Mark 9^{19} = Matt. 17^{17} = Luke 9^{41}; Mark 13^{24,25} = Matt. 24^{29} = Luke 21^{25,26} (p. 66), that characteristic forms of parallelism standing in Matthew (and in the last two cases in Mark and Matthew) are so modified in Luke as to destroy their form. The substance of the saying is there, but not its characteristically Semitic form of presentation. It surely follows from this fact that to Luke with his Greek training the Synonymous and Antithetical forms of parallelism appeared in some cases at least to exhibit a redundancy which was somewhat unattractive (or which he assumed would be unattractive to the Gentile circles for whom he wrote), and that for stylistic reasons he deliberately altered their form, while retaining their substance.[1] The alternative

[1] The objection of redundancy would naturally not be felt in the case of sayings cast in Synthetic parallelism, in which the sense is continuous, without repetition; and accordingly we are not, in the

theory would be that the Jewish editor of Matthew constructed parallelistic couplets out of single simple statements; but against this stands the fact that Matthew's Synonymous and Antithetic couplets can be paralleled in form from Mark, John, and by no means infrequently from Luke, so that the probability that they preserve the original form in which they stood in Q is high. If this reasoning is sound, we must assign to Matthew the palm for having (at least in such cases as can be tested by this criterion) preserved the sayings of Q in a more original form than Luke. It must be added that it does not follow that Matthew is superior in the order and setting of his materials; for naturally, while preserving the sayings intact, he may have rearranged them in accordance with the scheme which he had in view.

One more point needs to be added under this head. In two of the passages above cited in which Luke's version obliterates the Antithetic parallelism of Matthew, viz. Matt. $6^{19,20}$ = Luke 12^{33}; Matt. $7^{13,14}$ = Luke 13^{24}, we find that Luke's version exhibits a form of *rhythm* agreeable to the rhythm of the context,[1] and that in both cases the context is different from that of Matthew. This suggests the possibility that in these examples both Matthew and Luke may be original and accurate, our Lord having given the same teaching on different occasions in different form and setting.

case of Synthetic couplets, struck by marked alteration in Luke as compared with the other Synoptists; though even in these cases the test of *rhythm* suggests that Luke sometimes offers a less original *order* of words. Cf. Mark 2^{19-22} = Matt. 9^{15-17} = Luke 5^{34-9} (p. 140); Mark 13^{9-13} = Matt. 10^{17-22} = Luke 21^{12-17} (pp. 118, 119).

[1] Cf. p. 76.

Synthetic Parallelism.

In Synthetic or Constructive parallelism, as we noticed when speaking of the poetry of the Old Testament, the second line of a couplet neither repeats nor contrasts with the sense of the first, but the sense flows on continuously, much as in prose. There is, however, a correspondence between line and line of the couplet which marks them as the parts of a whole. This appears both in *sense*, the second line completing or supplementing the first, and also in *form*, the two lines balancing one another, and being commonly marked by identity of *rhythm*. Illustrations of this form of parallelism will be given when we deal with rhythm. At present it will suffice to quote a few examples.

Matt. 23^{5-10}.

'They make broad their phylacteries,
And enlarge their fringes.

And love the chief place at the feasts,
And the chief seats in the synagogues,

And the salutations in the market-places,
And to be called of men, Rabbi.

But be not ye called Rabbi
For one is your teacher,
And all ye are brethren.

And call no man your father on earth;
For One is your Father, the heavenly.

Neither be ye called masters;
For One is your Master, even Christ.'[1]

[1] Here it may be suspected that ὁ οὐράνιος, ὁ Χριστός are explicative additions.

Luke 12^{49-51}.

'I came to cast fire upon the earth;
And what will I, if it be already kindled?

But I have a baptism wherewith to be baptized,
And how am I straitened till it be accomplished!

Think ye that I came to give peace on the earth?
Nay, I tell you, but rather division.'

Here the last couplet is antithetic.

John 8^{44}.

'Ye are of your father, the devil,
And the lusts of your father ye will do.

He was a manslayer from the beginning,
And stood not in the truth.
[Because the truth is not in him.]

When he speaketh lying,
He speaketh of his own;

For he is a liar,
And the father of it.'[1]

Step-Parallelism.

We may give the name of Step-parallelism to a form of parallelism somewhat freely used by our Lord, in which a second line takes up a thought contained in the first line, and, repeating it, makes it as it were a step upwards for the development of a further thought, which is commonly the climax of the whole. Thus the parallelism is neither wholly Synonymous nor wholly Synthetic, but is partly Synonymous (or rather Identical) and partly Synthetic. This form of

[1] The square brackets mark the line as possibly an explicative addition.

parallelism, while occurring fairly often in the Synoptists, is especially frequent in the Fourth Gospel; and the fact that there should exist this resemblance between John and the Synoptists in so subtle a form of connexion, which would hardly be likely to be copied by an imitator of the latter, may be regarded as an important point in favour of the authenticity of the Johannine discourses. In the examples which follow we have italicized the term or phrase common to the stichoi, placing a perpendicular line before the climatic conclusion.

Mark 9^{37} = Matt. 18^{5} = Luke 9^{48}.

'He that receiveth this child in My name, *receiveth Me*;
And he that receiveth Me, | receiveth Him that sent Me.'

Besides this occurrence from M, we have the following similar sayings from Q and John:

Matt. 10^{40}.

'He that receiveth you, *receiveth Me*;
And he that receiveth Me, | receiveth Him that sent Me.'

Luke 10^{16}.

'He that heareth you, heareth Me;
And he that rejecteth you, *rejecteth Me*;
And he that rejecteth Me, | rejecteth Him that sent Me.'

John 13^{20}.

'He that receiveth whomsoever I shall send, *receiveth Me*;
And he that receiveth Me, | receiveth Him that sent Me.'

The following other examples come from Q:

Matt. 6^6.

'Pray to *thy Father that seeth in secret*;
And thy Father that seeth in secret | shall reward thee openly.'

Matt. 6^{22} = Luke 11^{34}.

'The light of the body is *the eye*;
If the eye | be single, &c.'

Matt. 6^{34}.

'Therefore be not anxious for *the morrow*;
For the morrow | shall be anxious for itself.'

Matt. 12^{39} = Luke 11^{29}.

'An evil and adulterous generation seeketh *a sign*;
And a sign | shall not be given it save the sign of Jonah the prophet.'[1]

Luke 12^5.

'But I will forewarn you whom *ye shall fear*:
Fear | Him who after He hath killed, &c.'[2]

Somewhat different, as embodying an antithesis, but still framed on the same principle are:

Matt. 5^{17}.

'Think not that *I came to destroy* the Law and the Prophets;
I came not to destroy, | but to fulfil.'

Matt. 10^{34}.

'Think not that *I came to bring peace* upon earth;
I came not to bring peace, | but a sword.'[3]

[1] Cf. Matt. 16^4 = Mark 8^{12}, where Mark phrases somewhat differently.

[2] Matt. 10^{28} omits the first line.

[3] Luke 12^{51} gives as the second line:

'Nay, I tell you, but rather division.'

This seems to be another illustration of the way in which he removes Semitic redundancy.

Coming now to the Fourth Gospel, we have the following illustrations of this form of parallelism :

John 6[37].

'Every one that the Father giveth Me *shall come to Me*;
And him that cometh to Me | I will in no wise cast out.'

John 8[32].

'And ye shall know *the truth*,
And the truth | shall make you free.'

John 10[11].

'I am *the good shepherd*;
The good shepherd | giveth His life for the sheep.'

John 11[25].

'*He that believeth on Me*, though he were dead, *shall live*;
And he that liveth and believeth on Me | shall never die.'

John 14[2,3].

'*I go to prepare a place for you.*
And if I go and prepare a place for you, |
I will come again and receive you unto Myself.'

John 14[21].

'He that hath My commandments and keepeth them, *he it is that loveth Me*;
But he that loveth Me | shall be loved of My Father.'

John 15[13,14].

'Greater love hath no man than this,
That a man lay down his life for his *friends*.
Ye are My *friends*, | if ye do whatsoever I command you.'

John 16^{7}.

'It is expedient for you that *I go away*;
For if I go not away, | the Comforter will not come unto you.'

John 16^{20}.

'Ye *shall be sorrowful*;
But your sorrow | shall become joy.'

John 16^{22}.

'Your heart shall *rejoice*,
And your joy | no one taketh from you.'

This form of development of a thought by recapitulation of it can also sometimes be traced where there is no parallelistic form, but where our Lord may be said to be speaking in prose.

John 10^{26,27}.

'But ye believe not because ye are not of *My sheep*. *My sheep* hear My voice, &c.'

John 18^{36}.

'*My kingdom is not of this world. If My kingdom were of this world*, then would My servants fight, &c.'

This form of recapitulation imparts a peculiar explicitness to the sayings so recorded.

In passing from the Fourth Gospel, we can hardly fail to note the striking fact that, in so far as this observation of connexion in form between sayings recorded by the Synoptists and by John may be held to lend weight to the authentication of the latter, it serves to authenticate some of the most precious sayings contained in this Gospel.

The form of parallelism which we have been examining might be termed *Climactic*, had not this term been already appropriated for a divergent and somewhat rare form of O.T. parallelism which is noted by Dr. Driver in his *Introduction to the Literature of the O.T.*[9], p. 363. In our Gospel-illustrations the first line in a couplet is usually *complete as regards sense*, and might conceivably stand by itself without the development in thought involved in the second line. In the O.T. examples of parallelism which is termed Climactic the sense of the first line is *incomplete*, and is only made complete by the second line. Thus:

Ps. 29^{1}.

'*Give unto Yahweh*, O ye sons of the mighty,
Give unto Yahweh | glory and strength.'

Ps. 92^{9}.

'*For behold, Thine enemies*, Yahweh,
For behold, Thine enemies | shall perish.'

Cf. also Ps. 93^{3}, 94^{3}, 96^{13}, 113^{1}, and the instances from the Song of Deborah collected by the present writer in his *Commentary on Judges*, p. 170. One of Dr. Driver's instances is, however, like our Gospel-parallelism.

Exod. 15^{16}.

'*Till Thy people pass over*, Yahweh,
Till Thy people pass over | which Thou hast purchased.'

Cf. also *vv.* [6, 11] of the same triumph-song.

A closer parallel is to be found in one of the 'Songs of Ascents':

Ps. 121.

'I will lift up my eyes unto the hills.
From whence cometh *my help*?
My help is from Yahweh,
Maker of heaven and earth.

He will not suffer thy foot to be moved;
Thy Keeper will not slumber.

Behold, *He will not slumber* nor sleep,
The Keeper of Israel.

Yahweh is thy *Keeper*,
Yahweh is thy shade upon thy right hand.

By day the sun shall not smite thee,
Neither the moon by night.

Yahweh shall keep thee from all ill;
He shall keep thy soul.

Yahweh shall keep thy going out and thy coming in
From henceforth and for ever.'

The most favoured theory as to the meaning of the term 'Songs of Ascents' is that the 'Ascents' are the periodical goings-up to Jerusalem for the festivals, and that the expression is equivalent to 'Pilgrim-songs'. Another suggestion, however, is that the 'Ascents' or 'Steps' refer to the step-like structure which we have noted in Ps. 121, and which may be traced in a less degree in most (though not in all) of the other Psalms which bear this title. Whether this be so or not, the view may serve to suggest the title 'Step-parallelism' as appropriate to the phenomenon which we have noted in the sayings of our Lord.

A further point of connexion between the Fourth Gospel and the Synoptists.

Before leaving the subject of parallelism, we may notice a characteristic of sayings in the Fourth Gospel which seems to find its analogue in the Synoptists. It frequently happens in John that a parallel couplet, of whatever class, is followed by a single line, taking the form of explanation of the couplet, development of its thought, or deduction from it. This single line may be regarded as turning the parallel distich into a tristich; or, as it is often of unequal length, as a prose-comment upon it. In the following examples the comment following the couplet is italicized:

John 3^{11}.

'That which we know we speak,
And that which we have seen we testify;
Yet ye receive not our testimony.'

John 3^{14}.

'As Moses lifted up the serpent in the wilderness,
So must the Son of man be lifted up;
That every one that believeth on Him may have everlasting life.'

John 3^{18}.

'He that believeth on Him is not condemned;
He that believeth not is already condemned,
Because he hath not believed on the name of the only-begotten Son of God.'

John 3^{19}.

'And this is the judgment:
Light is come into the world,
And men loved darkness rather than light,
Because their deeds were evil.'

John 3^{34}.

'He whom God hath sent
Speaketh the words of God;
For not in measure giveth He the Spirit.

The Father loveth the Son,
And hath given all things into His hand.

He that believeth on the Son hath everlasting life;
But he that disbelieveth the Son shall not see life,
But the wrath of God abideth on him.'

John 4^{22}.

'Ye worship ye know not what;
We know what we worship;
For salvation is of the Jews.'

John 4^{36}.

'He that reapeth receiveth wages,
And gathereth fruit unto life eternal;
That both the sower and the reaper may rejoice together.'

John 6^{32}.

'Verily, verily I say unto you,
Not Moses gave you the bread from heaven,
But My Father giveth you the true bread from heaven;
For the bread of God is He that cometh down from heaven, and giveth life to the world.'

On first noticing this characteristic, the writer's impression was that, assuming the parallel couplet to be a genuine saying of our Lord, the comment following might be due to the author of the Gospel. Later, however, he detected precisely the same characteristic in some of the sayings recorded by the Synoptists. The following are examples:

Mark 2^{27}.

'The sabbath was made for man,
And not man for the sabbath;
So that the Son of man is lord even of the sabbath.'[1]

[1] Matt. 12^{8}, Luke 6^{5} give the deduction merely, unpreceded by the antithetic couplet.

Luke 11^{34}.

'The light of the body is the eye;
When thine eye is single,
Thy whole body is light;
But when it is evil,
Thy body also is dark.
Take heed therefore lest the light that is in thee be darkness.' [1]

Matt. 6^{24} = Luke 16^{13}.

'No steward can serve two masters;
For either he will hate the one and love the other,
Or he will hold to the one and despise the other.
Ye cannot serve God and mammon.'

Matt. 12^{33} = Luke 6^{43}.

'Either make the tree good and its fruit good,
Or make the tree bad and its fruit bad;
For from the fruit is the tree known.' [2]

Luke 6^{45}.

'The good man out of the good treasure of his heart bringeth forth good,
And the evil man out of the evil bringeth forth evil;
For out of the abundance of the heart the mouth speaketh.' [3]

[1] In Matt. $6^{22, 23}$ we read:

'If then the light that is in thee be darkness,
How great is that darkness!'

This may be regarded as a couplet, which may be more original than the Lucan form.

[2] Luke runs somewhat differently from Matt.:

'A good tree bringeth not forth bad fruit,
Nor again doth a bad tree bring forth good fruit;
For every tree is known by its own fruit.'

[3] The comment is lacking in Matt. 12^{35}.

III

THE USE OF RHYTHM BY OUR LORD

In speaking of our Lord's use of rhythm, it is well to begin with a word of caution. The employment of rhythm in poetical composition naturally involves some amount of artifice, and, *for its perfection*, usually demands from the poet thought and labour. We may regard the Psalms as poems upon which a good deal of labour was expended by their authors in working them into poetical form. The Prophets, on the other hand, we picture as uttering their oracles to a large extent without previous preparation; and it seems obvious that they must have done so when speaking on the spur of the moment under the sudden access of the Divine afflatus. Yet their most impassioned oracles, which (so far as we can judge) would be spoken most directly under sudden inspiration, are usually those which exhibit most clearly the characteristics of Hebrew poetry; and it is obvious that they must have possessed wonderful powers of poetical improvisation. We should naturally expect, however, to find the prophetic oracles less rhythmically perfect than are most of the Psalms; even though it be possible that, when a prophecy came to be committed to writing, the prophet may have aimed at making it more formally perfect as a poetical composition than it was when he first improvised it. If the telling phrase which leaped to his mind on the spur of the moment would not fit into his rhythm, we cannot suppose that he would have rejected it on that account; nor in subsequent revision (if this took place) can we think that he would have cared to improve it away in favour of some expression less telling but more rhythmically perfect. As a fact, we *do* find less rhythmical perfection in the prophetic oracles than, e.g., in the Psalms or in Job; yet this occasional rhythmical roughness does not, on the one hand, indicate that they are not to be taken as poetical compositions; nor, on the other hand, on the assumption that they *are* poetry, does it justify us in emending them to produce a dead level of rhythmical uniformity, as is attempted by many modern Hebrew scholars. They *are* poetry without a doubt, in form no less than in thought, albeit that their rhythm may sometimes fail of perfection, and that they may exhibit quick alternation from one form of rhythm to another. It may be questioned, indeed, whether perfect rhythmical regularity was regarded by the Hebrews as a poetical merit. We rarely find it, even in the Psalms.[1]

In maintaining that our Lord was accustomed with some frequency to cast His teaching into rhythmical

[1] These remarks must not be taken as implying that it is illegitimate to emend the text of Old Testament poems and prophetic oracles by the help of rhythmical considerations. It constantly happens that, in passages where the Hebrew text is rhythmically at fault, the sense of the passage is also obscure, or defies the rules of Hebrew grammar or usage; and in such cases the original can often be plausibly conjectured so as to restore regularity of rhythm. Some amount of emendation has been made by the writer on rhythmical grounds in the renderings given in Chap. I as illustrations of different forms of Hebrew rhythm. The *caveat* is only lodged against the unwarrantable assumption that a Hebrew poem or oracle always must exhibit unimpeachable regularity throughout.

forms identical with those employed by the Hebrew poets and prophets of the Old Testament, we are met by two initial difficulties. In the first place, whereas in the Old Testament we have the Hebrew originals before us, in the Gospels we are dependent merely upon translations of the original utterances, and can therefore only substantiate our case by retranslation into the assumed Aramaic original. And secondly, while the forms of Hebrew rhythm can be substantiated by a multitude of examples, the work of various authors, which are mutually confirmatory, in dealing with our Lord's sayings we suffer from a lack of similarly constructed teaching in Aramaic, which might prove that Hebrew rhythmical methods were employed in the sister-language.

These difficulties admitted, it may still be maintained that our thesis can be proved. We are dependent upon Greek translations of our Lord's sayings; yet, as the preceding chapter has shown, this does not hinder us in the slightest degree from observing that our Lord used forms of *parallelism* in all respects like those of the Old Testament, since parallelism, being inherent in the form and substance of the saying, is as apparent in translation as in the original language of the speaker. Now the fact can scarcely escape notice that there is a close relation between parallelism and rhythm. This is particularly noticeable in Synonymous parallelism, in which, in its most typical forms, stichos *b* of a couplet repeats stichos *a* term for term in varying language. To take a few examples:

Ps. 19[2].

'Day	unto day	uttereth	speech,
And night	unto night	sheweth	knowledge.'

Ps. 94^{9}.

'He that planted	the ear,	shall He not hear?
Or He that formed	the eye,	shall He not see?'

Num. 23^{8}.

How can I curse	whom God	hath not cursed?
And how can I denounce	whom Yahweh	hath not denounced?'

In each of these couplets we have in the parallel stichoi an accurate correspondence between member and member which carries with it correspondence in rhythm. When, then, we observe among our Lord's sayings instances of Synonymous parallelism which are precisely similar, i.e. in which the parallel lines exhibit term-for-term correspondence, the conclusion is inevitable that there must have existed an identity of rhythm in the parallel stichoi at least as apparent in the original Aramaic as it is in the English rendering of the Greek form of the sayings. Examples are:

Matt. 7^{6}.

'Give not	the holy thing	to the dogs,
And cast not	your pearls	before swine.'

Matt. 23^{29}.

'Ye build	the sepulchres	of the prophets,
And adorn	the tombs	of the righteous.'

John 3^{11}.

'That which	we know	we speak,
And that which	we have seen	we testify.'

John 6^{35}.

'He that cometh	to Me	shall never hunger,
And he that believeth	on Me	shall never thirst.'

John 13^{16}.

'The servant	is not greater	than his lord,
And the messenger	is not greater	than him that sent him.'

John 20^{27}.

'Stretch out hither	thy finger,	and behold	My hands;
And stretch out	thy hand,	and put (it)	into My side

In the most typical form of Antithetic parallelism the case is similar, term answering to term in the contrasted statements of the parallel lines.

Ps. 20^{8} (Heb.^{9}).

'*They*	are bowed down	and fallen,
But *we*	are risen	and stand upright.'

Prov. 10^{7}.

'The memory	of the righteous	is blessed,
But the name	of the wicked	shall rot.'

Prov. 12^{5}.

'The plans	of the righteous	are justice,
The designs	of the wicked	are deceit.'

Of precisely similar construction are many of the antithetical sayings of our Lord. The following may be cited as examples:

Matt. 7^{17}.

'Every good tree	bringeth forth	good fruits,
But the corrupt tree	bringeth forth	evil fruits.'

Matt. 23^{12}.

'Whoso exalteth	himself	shall be abased,
But he that humbleth	himself	shall be exalted.'

Mark 7^{8}.

'Forsaking	the commandment	of God,
Ye hold	the tradition	of men.'

Luke 16^{10}.

He that is faithful | in little, | is faithful | in much;
And he that is dishonest | in little, | is dishonest | in much.'

John 3^{6}.

'That which is born | of the flesh | is flesh,
And that which is born | of the spirit | is spirit.'

Such term-for-term correspondence in Synonymous parallelism is by no means, however, uniformly characteristic of this form of parallelism. It frequently happens, as mentioned in the opening chapter (p. 17), that some one member of the first stichos (especially a verb) may extend its influence into the second stichos, which thus possesses no synonym to form an equivalent rhythmical balance. In such a case it is commonly found that the equivalent in stichos *b* of one of the other terms in stichos *a* is *a compound one*, offering two stress-accents, and thus redressing the rhythmical balance. Examples are:

Ps. 24^{5}.

He shall receive | a blessing | from Yahweh
| And righteousness | from the God | of his salvation.'

Here, if we denote the terms of the first stichos by *a*, *b*, *c*, those of the second will be denoted by *b*, c^{2}.

Ps. 15^{1}.

'Yahweh, | who shall sojourn | in Thy tent?
| Who shall rest | on Thy holy | hill?'

Here again the notation is *a*, *b*, *c*; *b*, c^{2}.

Amos 5^{24}.

And let roll down | like water | justice,
| And righteousness | like a stream | unfailing.'

Notation, *a*, *b*, *c*; *c*, b^{2}.

This rhythmical equivalence by compensation may be illustrated from our Lord's sayings.

Matt. 8^{20}.

'The foxes | possess | holes,
The birds | of the heavens | | nests.'

Notation, *a*, *b*, *c*; a^2, *c*.

Mark 13^{25}.

'The stars | shall fall | from heaven,
And the powers | in the heavens | shall be shaken.'

Notation, *a*, b^2; a^2, *b*.

John 6^{26}.

'Ye seek Me, | not because ye saw | signs,
| But because ye ate | of the loaves | and were satisfied
Labour not | for the food | which perisheth,
| But for the food | which abideth | unto life eternal.'

Notation, *a*, *b*, *c*; *b*, *c*, *d*: *a*, *b*, *c*; *b*, c^2.

John 4^{36}.

'He that reapeth | receiveth | wages,
| And gathereth | fruit | unto life eternal.'

Notation, *a*, *b*, *c*; *b*, *c*, *d*.[1]

[1] It may be objected to the citation of these two passages from John to illustrate the point at issue, that the phrase 'unto life eternal', in Aramaic presumably *l^{e}ḥayyîn dil'ālam*, ought, according to the rules laid down for Hebrew rhythm on pp. 43 ff., to bear two rhythmical stresses and not one only. In answer, the writer can only record his instinct that it should, in the passages in question, represent one stress merely (cf. the somewhat analogous cases cited under § 7 of the rules, p. 55). Thus regarded, it is not more forced than the one-stress 'Withouten any pénaunce' in the passage from *Piers Plowman* cited on p. 28. It is possible, however, that the original of both passages may have read 'unto life' simply (cf. *ch.* $3^{36\,b}$, $5^{24\,b,\ 29,\ 40}$, $6^{33,\ 53,\ 63}$, 10^{10}, Mark $9^{43,\ 45}$, Matt. 7^{14}, 19^{17}), or that in John 6^{27} the phrase may have been 'for ever' (lit. 'to eternity', expanded into 'to life which is to eternity').

We may now observe the occasional occurrence in our Lord's discourses of *quatrains* in which there exist Synonymous or Antithetic parallelism, not between successive lines, but between alternate lines, stichos *a* being thus parallel to stichos *c*, and stichos *b* to stichos *d*.

Synonymous quatrain:

Luke 12^{43}.

'To whomsoever	is given	much,
Of him	much	shall be required;
And to whom	they commit	much,
The more	shall they ask	of him.'

Antithetic quatrains:

Matt. $6^{14,15}$.

'If ye forgive	to men	their trespasses,
Your Father	in heaven	shall forgive you;
But if ye forgive not	to men	their trespasses,
Neither shall your Father	forgive	your trespasses.'

John $3^{20,21}$.

Every doer	of ill	hateth	the light,
And cometh not	to the light	lest his works	be condemned;
But the worker	of the truth	cometh to	the light
That his deeds	may be manifest	as wrought	in God.'

John 11^{9}.

'If one walk	in the day	he stumbleth not,
For the light	of this world	he seeth;
But if one walk	in the night	he stumbleth,
For the light	is not	in him.'

Examples of similarly constructed quatrains in Hebrew poetry are the following:

Ps. $33^{13,14}$.

'From heaven	looketh	Yahweh,
He beholdeth	all the children	of men.
From the place	of His seat	He gazeth
Upon all	the inhabitants	of the earth.

Ps. $103^{11, 12}$.

'As the heavens	are high	o'er the earth,
His kindness	is great	o'er His fearers;
As the east	is remote	from the west,
He hath removed	from us	our transgressions.'

Ps. 127^{1}.

'If Yahweh	build not	the house,
In vain	do labour	its builders;
If Yahweh	watch not	the city,
In vain	doth wake	the watchman.'

Now while in these sayings of Christ there clearly exists Synonymous or Antithetic parallelism between stichoi *a* and *c* and between stichoi *b* and *d*, which carries with it an identity of rhythmical balance, it is no less evident that there also exists a similar relation of rhythmical balance between stichoi *a* and *b* and between stichoi *c* and *d*; although, since the sense runs on from *a* to *b* and from *c* to *d* and is not repeated either synonymously or antithetically, the parallelism is of the kind which in Hebrew poetry we class as *Synthetic*. The whole quatrains in fact are characterized by identity of rhythm in every line, this rhythm taking the form of three beats to the line in three of the examples, and four beats to the line in the remaining one. The proved existence of rhythmical Synthetic parallelism in these examples may be held to substantiate the reasonableness of the claim that this form of rhythmical parallelism is also to be traced in other examples in which it does not alternate in the same regular manner with Synonymous or Antithetic parallelism, but in which the whole passage appears to be more or less continuously of a Synthetic character, as happens with considerable frequency in Hebrew poetry. The proof that this is so must depend upon study of the illustrations which we shall presently proceed to cite.

Passing to our second difficulty—the lack of literature in Aramaic of our Lord's time or somewhat earlier which might substantiate the hypothesis that this language employed the rhythmical methods of Hebrew poetry—we observe that, sparse indeed as are the survivals of such literature, we are not altogether without the desired proof. The Aramaic section of the Book of Daniel (*chs.* $2^{4b}-7^{28}$) contains a considerable amount of matter which is cast in poetical form, exhibiting both parallelism and rhythm precisely of the same character as that which is found in Hebrew poetry. We may note the following examples :

Dan. 4^3 (Aram. 3^{33}).
'ātôhī k^{e}mấ rabr^{e}bín
w^{e}timhôhī k^{e}mấ takkīphín
malkūtéh malkút 'ālắm
w^{e}šoltānéh 'im dắr w^{e}dắr

'His sígns how exceéding greát!
And His wónders how exceéding míghty!
His kíngdom is a kíngdom of etérnity,
And His domínion from generátion to generátion.'

Dan. $4^{11,12}$ (Aram. ^{8,9}).
r^{e}bấ 'ilānấ ūt^{e}ḳíph
w^{e}rūméh yimṭḗ lišmayyấ
waḥ^{a}zōtéh l^{e}sôph kol 'ar'ấ
'ophyéh šappír w^e'inbéh saggí
ūmāzốn l^{e}kôllā béh
t^{e}ḥōtôhī taṭlḗl ḥēwát bārấ
ūb^e'anphôhī y^{e}dúrān ṣipp^{e}rḗ š^{e}mayyấ
ūminnéh yitt^{e}zín kol bisrấ

'The treé grew greát and waxed stróng,
And its height attaíned to the heávens,

And its síght to the énd of the whole eárth.
Its leáves were faír and its fruít was múch,
And foód for áll was ín it;
Under it shéltered the beásts of the fiéld,
And in its bránches dwélt the bírds of the heávens,
And fróm it all flésh was féd.'

Dan. 4[14] (Aram. [11])

gṓddū 'īlānā́ wᵉḳaṣṣíṣū ʿanpṓhī
'attárū ʿophyḗh ūbaddárū 'inbḗh
tᵉnū́d ḥēwᵉtā́ min tᵉḥōtṓhī
wᵉṣíppᵉrayyā́ min ʿanpṓhī

'Héw down the treé and lóp off its bránches;
Sháke off its leáves and scátter its fruít;
Let the beásts get awáy from únder it,
And álso the bírds from its bránches.'

Dan. 4[17] (Aram. [14]).

bigzērát ʿīrī́n pitgāmā́
ūmēmár ḳaddīšī́n šᵉ'ēltā́

'By the decreé of the wátchers is the séntence,
And ⟨by⟩ the wórd of the hóly ones is the mátter.'

Dan. 4[27] (Aram. [24]).

lāhēn malkā
milkī́ yišpár ʿᵃlā́k
waḥᵃṭā'ā́k bᵉṣidḳā́ pᵉrū́ḳ,
waʿᵃwāyātā́k bᵉmiḥán ʿᵃnā́yin
hēn tehᵉwḗ 'arkā́ lišlēwᵉtā́k

'Wherefore, O king,
Be my coúnsel accéptable únto thee;
And thy síns by ríghteousness break óff,
And thine iníquities by pítying the poór;
It may bé a léngthening to thy tranquíllity.

The greater part of this chapter appears to be constructed in a more or less regular rhythmical form.

Dan. 5^{10}.

'al y^e^bah^a^lū́k ra'yōnā́k
w^e^zīwā́k 'ál yištannṓ

'Lét not thy thoúghts troúble thee
And lét not thy coúntenance be chánged.'

Dan. 5^{17}.

matt^e^nātā́k lā́k lehewyā́n
ūn^e^bozb^e^yātā́k l^e^'oḥ^o^rān háb
b^e^ram k^e^tābā́ 'eḳrḗ l^e^malkā́
ūphišrā́ ' hṓd^e^'innḗh

'Let thy gífts belóng to thysélf,
And thy rewárds to anóther gíve;
Yet the wríting will I reád to the kíng,
And the meáning to hím will make knówn.'

Dan. $5^{20,21}$.

ūk^e^dī́ rī́m lib^e^bḗh
w^e^rūḥḗh tiḳphát lah^a^zādā́
honḥát min korsḗ malkūtḗh
wīḳārā́ hé'dī́w minnḗh
ūmin b^e^nḗ '^e^nāšā́ ṭ^e^rī́d
w^e^lib^e^bḗh 'im ḥēw^e^tā́ šawwī́w
w^e^'im '^a^rā́dayyā́ m^e^dōrḗh
'isbā́ k^e^tōrī́n y^e^ṭa'^a^mūnḗh
ūmiṭṭál š^e^mayyā́ [gišmḗh] yiṣṭabbá'
'ad dī y^e^da'
dī šallī́ṭ [^e^lāhā́] 'illā'ā́ b^e^malkū́t '^e^nāšā́
ūl^e^mán dī yiṣbḗ y^e^hāḳḗm '^a^láh [1]

[1] For omission of *gišmēh*, cf. $4^{12, 22}$ (it is found in 4^{30}). For omission of *'^e^lāhā*, cf. $4^{14, 22, 29}$.

'But whén his heárt was exálted,
And his spírit grew stróng to act proúdly,
He was depósed from the thróne of his kíngdom,
And the glóry was táken fróm him.
And from the sóns of mén was he chásed,
And his heárt with the beásts was lévelled,
And wíth the wild ásses was his dwélling;
With gráss like óxen was he féd,
And with the déw of heáven [his bódy] was wétted;
Until he knew
That the Most Hígh [God] is rúler in the kíngdom of mankínd,
And whomsoéver He wíll He appoínteth óver it.'

When investigating the formally poetical character of our Lord's sayings, we must not—any more than in the oracles of the Old Testament prophets—expect to find perfect rhythmical regularity maintained throughout lengthy passages. It will suffice to prove the case if the Hebrew forms of rhythm are found to be exhibited over short passages, and exhibited with alternations and occasional irregularities.

Four-beat rhythm.

The first example of this which we shall take is the Lord's Prayer as given in Matt. 6[9-13]:

'Our Fáther in heáven, hállowed be Thy náme.
Thy kíngdom cóme; Thy wíll be dóne,
Ás in the heávens, só on eárth.

Our daíly (?) breád gíve us to-dáy;
And forgíve us our débts, as we forgíve our débtors;
And leád us not into temptátion, but delíver us from évil.

Here we have, in fact, a little poem or hymn consisting of two four-beat tristichs. We see at once what an aid the rhythmical form is in assisting the memory. The formula may be said to be 2 (stanzas) × 3 (stichoi) × 4 (beats). Was it accidental that our Lord so composed it, or did He intentionally employ art in composition as an aid to memory? Surely the latter conclusion is correct. Comparing this form of the prayer with the mutilated version which we find in the Revisers' text of Luke 11^{2-4}, we can hardly hesitate as to which is the more original.

The prayer may be translated into Galilaean Aramaic as follows:

'ᵃbūnán dᵉbišmayyā́   *yitḳaddáš šᵉmā́k*
tētḗ malkūtā́k   *tᵉhḗ ṣibyōnā́k*
hēkmā́ dᵉbišmayyā́   *hēkdḗn bᵉ'ạr'ā́*

laḥmán dᵉyōmā́   *hab lán yōmā dḗṇ*
ūšᵉbōḳ lán ḥōbḗn   *hēk dišbáḳnan lᵉḥayyābḗn*
wᵉlā ta'lī́nan lᵉnisyōnā́   *'ellā paṣṣī́nan miṇ bīšā́*

We will now take a number of other passages from Q in which Matthew's version is contained in the Sermon on the Mount, but in which we shall find that Luke's version more regularly employs this rhythm, and also exhibits further connected teaching which is not found in Matthew. We shall therefore take the Lucan form as typical.

Luke 6^{27-29}.

'But I say unto you that hear,
Lóve your énemies,   do goód to your háters,
Bléss your cúrsers,   práy for your revílers.

To thy stríker on the cheék offer the óther,
And from the táker of thy clóke withhóld not thy coát.'[1]

Luke 6^{36-38}.

'Bé ye mérciful, as your Fáther is mérciful.
Júdge not, that ye be not júdged; condémn not, that ye be not condémned;
Releáse, and ye shall be releásed; gíve, and it shall be gíven you;
Goódly meásure, préssed, sháken,
Overflówing ⟨. . .⟩ shall they gíve into your bósom.
For with what meásure ye méte it shall be meásured to yóu.'[2]

Luke $11^{9,10}$ = Matt. $7^{7,8}$.

'Ásk, and it shall be gíven you;
Seék, and ye shall fínd;
Knóck, and it shall be ópened to you.

[1] Matt. 5^{44} = Luke $6^{27a, 28b}$ (with διωκόντων for ἐπηρεαζόντων) exhibits the same rhythm. The omitted clauses of Luke are found in the Western text in reverse order to that of Luke. Matt. $5^{39b, 40}$ = Luke 6^{29}. The most important differences, so far as rhythm is concerned, are the insertion of 'right' before 'cheek', and the reading 'from him that wisheth to judge thee and take' in place of 'from the taker of'. These differences spoil the rhythm of Luke, whose text must, on this criterion, be judged more original.

[2] Matt. 5^{48} = Luke 6^{36}, with τέλειοι . . . τέλειος in place of οἰκτίρμονες . . . οἰκτίρμων, and 'heavenly' before 'Father'. Matt. 7^{1} = Luke 6^{37a} (to 'judged'), Luke 6^{38b} ('For with what measure, &c.') = Matt. 7^{2b} (cf. also Mark 4^{24}). The remainder is unparalleled in Matthew. In the half-stichos 'overflowing' we seem to need some parallel term to complete the rhythm, unless, as is quite possible, 'overflowing' was expressed in two words in Aramaic, e.g. 'running outside'.

For every ásker receíveth;
And the seéker fíndeth;
And to the knócker it shall be ópened.'[1]

Luke 12^{32-37}.

'Fear not, little flock,

For it pleáseth your Fáther	to gíve you the kíngdom.
Séll your goóds,	and gíve álms;
Máke yourselves scríps	that wáx not óld,
A treásure in heáven	that néver faíleth,
Where no thiéf approácheth	nor móth corrúpteth;
For whére your treásure,	thére your heárt.
Let your loíns be gírt,	and your lámps búrning,
And yé like mén	awaíting their lórd,
Whén he shall retúrn	from the márriage-feást;
that cóming and knócking,	at ónce they may ópen to him.

Bléssed those sérvants
Whom the lórd, when he cómeth,
Shall fínd wátching.'[2]

[1] Matthew and Luke are substantially identical.

[2] The equivalent of Luke $12^{33, 34}$ is found in Matt. 6^{19-21}, which runs:

'Lay not up for yourselves treasures in earth,
Where moth and rust corrupteth,
And where thieves break through and steal;

But lay up for yourselves treasures in heaven,
Where neither moth nor rust corrupteth,
And where thieves break not through nor steal.

For where your treasure, there your heart.'

This (except for the last line, which = Luke's four-beat rhythm) seems to fall into three-beat rhythm, and is also cast in typical antithetic form. We should perhaps conclude from this that both the Luke and Matthew

Closely connected, though without a parallel in Matthew, is the following passage from Luke.

Luke $12^{42, 43}$.

‘Whó is the stéward	trústy and wíse,
Whom the lórd shall appoínt	óver his rétinue,
To gíve in seáson	the meásure of foód?

Bléssed that sérvant
Whom his lórd, when he cómeth
Shall fínd so dóing.’

We may compare the following passage from Matthew which is rhythmically similar.

Matt. 13^{52}.

‘Every scríbe that is apprénticed	to the kíngdom of heáven
Is líke to a mán	that is rúler of a hoúse,
Who brings fórth from his treásure	things néw and óld.’

In the following passage Matthew and Luke are practically identical.

Matt. 6^{24} = Luke 16^{13}.

‘Nó one can sérve	twó másters.
Either he shall háte the óne	and lóve the óther,
Or shall hóld to the óne	and despíse the óther.
Ye cánnot sérve	Gód and Mámmon.’[1]

forms are original, but belong to different occasions. Luke $12^{35, 36}$ has no direct parallel in Matthew, but it may be noted that a parallel *in substance* is offered by the parable of the ten virgins (Matt. $25^{1 \text{ ff}}$.)—a fact which bears out the conclusion that our Lord sometimes repeated the same teaching in a different form on different occasions.

[1] The only difference is that Matthew's *οὐδείς* appears in Luke as *οὐδεὶς οἰκέτης*. Luke's addition, which is rhythmically superflous, is probably explicative.

Our Lord's commission to Peter, peculiar to Matthew, is cast in this rhythm, and falls into tristichs.

Matt. 16$^{17-19}$.

'Blessed thoú, Sim'ón,	thou són of Jonáh,
For flésh and bloód	reveáled not to theé,
Bút My Fáther	Who ís in heáven.

And I sáy unto theé	that thoú art Péter,
And upón this róck	I will buíld My chúrch,
And the gátes of Sheól	shall not prevaíl agaínst it.

I will gíve thee the kéys	of the kíngdom of heáven,
And that thou shalt bínd on éarth	shall be boúnd in heáven,
And that thou shalt loóse on eárth	shall be loósed in heáven.'

This may be thus rendered in Aramaic:

ṭūbáyk Šim'ṓn	*b^{e}rḗh d^{e}Yōnā́*
d^{e}bisrā́ ūd^{e}mā́	*lā gā́lē lā́k*
'ellā́ 'abbā́	*d^{e}'īt hū́ bišmayyā́*

w^{e}'āmárna lā́k	*d^{e}'att hū́ Kēphā́*
w^{e}'al hādḗn kēphā́	*'ebnḗ likništī́*
w^{e}tar'ḗh diš'ṓl	*lā yēk^{e}lū́n '^{a}lḗh*

'īhab lā́k mapht^{e}ḥayyā́	*d^{e}malkūtā́ dišmayyā́*
ūmā d^{e}tēsṓr b^{e}'ar'ā́	*yitt^{e}sár bišmayyā́*
ūmā d^{e}tišrḗ b^{e}'ar'ā́	*yišt^{e}rḗ bišmayyā́*

The reply sent to St. John Baptist is framed in the same rhythm.

Matt. 11$^{4-6}$ = Luke 7^{22,23}.

'Go ye and tell John what ye have seen and heard;

The blínd seé,	the láme wálk,
The lépers are cleánsed,	the deáf heár,
The deád are raísed,	the poór are evángelized;
And bléssed whosó	shall not stúmble in Mé.'

We may trace the same form of rhythm in M in *vv.* $^{9-13}$ of the little Apocalypse of Mark 13. This section is distinguished from the rest of the chapter by its rhythm. We have parallelism, and an imperfect rhythm of a different character, in *vv.* $^{8, 24-27}$, but the remainder is unmarked by the characteristics of Hebrew poetry.

Mark 13^{9-13}.

9.	'They shall delíver you unto coúncils,	and in sýnagogues shall ye be scoúrged,
	And before rúlers and kíngs	shall ye stánd for My sáke.
		[for a witness unto them.]
10.	[And unto all nations first	must the Gospel be preached.]
11.	And whén they arrést you	and delíver you úp,
	Be not ánxious befóre-hand	whát ye shall speák;
	But that gíven you at that hóur,	thát speák ye;
	For it is not yé that speák,	but the Hóly Spírit.
12.	And bróther shall betráy	bróther to deáth,
	[And father son,]	
	And chíldren shall rise úp	against párents and sláy them.
13.	And ye shall be háted of áll	for Mý name's sáke;
	But he that endúreth to the énd,	hé shall be sáved.'

The bracketed passages are imperfectly rhythmical, and their originality may therefore be suspected—εἰς μαρτύριον αὐτοῖς (*v.* ^{9}) and καὶ πατὴρ τέκνον (*v.* ^{12}) as being half-lines merely, and καὶ εἰς πάντα τὰ ἔθνη κτλ. (*v.* [10]) as having no parallel line. In confirmation of the omission of this latter passage we note that it introduces a fresh thought which interrupts the connexion between *v.* [9] and *v.* [11]. On removal of the bracketed passages we observe that we have a couplet (*v.* [9]) followed by two quatrains (*v.* [11] and *vv.* [12, 13]). This may lead us to suspect that the opening couplet is the half of an original quatrain, of the second half of which εἰς μαρτύριον αὐτοῖς may be a relic.

The parallel passage in Luke 21^{12-19} is so paraphrased as to remove all traces of rhythm, and is therefore, *in form*, less original. We notice, however, that it preserves the whole of the Marcan *matter*, except Mark 13^{10} καὶ εἰς πάντα τὰ ἔθνη κτλ.—the very passage which we have marked on rhythmical grounds as suspicious. A further parallel to Mark 13^{11} is found in Luke $12^{11,12}$; and this again is paraphrastic and unrhythmical.

Matt. 24^{9-14}, which should form a parallel to the passage under consideration, only does so very imperfectly; being unrhythmical, and, as compared with Mark, paraphrastic and disordered in sequence, and containing some new thoughts (e.g. *vv.* [11, 12]). The true parallel to Mark 13^{9-13} is found, however, in Matt. 10^{17-22}, which corresponds exactly in extent with the Marcan passage which we have distinguished from the rest of Mark 13 solely on the ground of rhythm. We may now observe that a further ground for distinction is to be found in its *contents*. Though not unsuited to be fitted into an eschatological discourse, the section is not in itself eschatological, but simply predicts the treatment which the Apostles and other members of the Church will receive from the world in the prosecution of their missionary work, and lays down rules for their conduct, independently of the thought of a speedy termination of the present age (unless we press the force of εἰς τέλος in *v.* 13, as there seems no need to do).[1] The setting of the passage in Matt. 10 is uneschatological, apart from *v.* 23b which alludes (though only incidentally) to the coming of the Son of Man. The whole chapter deals with the commission of the Twelve and the setting forth and implications of their apostolic work. This consideration seems at any rate to open the possibility that Matthew may have drawn 10^{17-22}, not directly from the little Apocalypse of Mark, but from another independent source; and since Matt. 10^{17-22} is practically identical with Mark 13^{9-13}, with but small variations (including the omission of Mark 13^{10} which we suspect on rhythmical grounds), and Mark 13^{9-13} is distinguished (as we have seen) from its context by a rhythm not traceable elsewhere in the chapter, and its removal from its context, so far from damaging the sequence of thought, improves it by connecting *v.* 8 directly with *v.* 14, a plausible inference seems to be that both Mark and Matthew drew the passage independently from an earlier common source (Q ?). This inference is confirmed when we notice that Luke, who follows Mark in his version of the little Apocalypse, must have felt that the section in question was logically misplaced; for he prefaces it with the words Πρὸ δὲ τούτων πάντων (21^{12}). On this view of the Marcan section we naturally regard the opening words of *v.* 9, Βλέπετε δὲ ὑμεῖς ἑαυτούς, as the redactional link by which Mark

[1] Matt. 24^{9-14}, which, as we have just noted, imperfectly represents Mark 13^{9-13}, though based upon it, has clearly been *made* eschatological in accordance with its context (the little Apocalypse in Matthew).

connects the passage with the context in which he places it.

Looking now at the context of Matt. 10^{17-22}, we observe that the section immediately preceding, viz. *vv.* $^{8-16}$, which contains a commission for missionary work, exhibits signs of the same form of rhythm. This is more clearly observable in the parallels Mark 6^{8-11}, Luke 9^{3-5}. The following reconstruction, which is necessarily somewhat tentative, is based mainly on Mark, though accepting Matt. 10^{8} (summarily paraphrased in Mark 6^{7b}, Luke 9^{1b}) and Matt. 10^{16} (cf. Luke 10^{3}) as illustrative of the same form of rhythm.[1]

[1] The divergence between the command of Mark 6^{8} to take nothing for the journey *except* a staff only, and Matt. 10^{10}, Luke 9^{3}, which specify *no* staff, is probably due to misreading of the Aramaic אֶלָּא, *'ellā*, 'but', as וְלָא, *w^elā*, 'and not', i.e. 'not even', which is not unnatural in view of the repeated לָא, 'not', in the list of forbidden articles which follows. (Allen on Mark 6^{9} regards וְלָא as original, and אֶלָּא as a corruption.) In Mark 6^{8} we restore the *oratio recta* as in the parallels, rejecting *καὶ ἔλεγεν αὐτοῖς* in *v.* ^{10}, and supplying in this verse Matthew's *ἀσπάσασθε αὐτήν*, 'Ask its peace' (welfare; cf. Luke 10^{5}, *εἰρήνη τῷ οἴκῳ τούτῳ*), as inherently probable and needful to complete the rhythm. The variants Mark 6^{11} *καὶ ὃς ἂν τόπος μὴ δέξηται ὑμᾶς*, Matt. 10^{14} *καὶ ὃς ἂν μὴ δέξηται ὑμᾶς*, Luke 9^{5} *καὶ ὅσοι ἂν μὴ δέχωνται ὑμᾶς*, are clearly different ways of filling out an original וּדְלָא מְקַבֵּל לְכוֹן, lit. 'and that receiveth you not', which may be taken naturally as referring to the 'house' preceding. This *casus pendens* may have been concisely reinforced by the pronominal suffix in עַפְרֵיהּ, 'its dust', the statements *ἐκπορευόμενοι ἐκεῖθεν, εἰς μαρτύριον αὐτοῖς* being added to make the sense clearer in the Greek. The fact that the section in Matthew has been expounded from the form preserved in Mark is indicated by the occurrence of most of its additions in a different context in Luke ($10^{5, 6, 12}$). The opening of the charge in Matt. 10^{5-7}, with its specific limitation of the mission to the lost sheep of the house of Israel, does not accord with the rhythm of the rest, and finds no parallel in Mark and Luke. It may perhaps be editorial, and not drawn from an earlier written source.

'Heál the síck,	raíse the deád,
Cleánse the lépers,	cást out dévils;
Freély ye have receíved,	freély gíve.
Take noúght for the joúrney	but stáff alóne,
No breád, no scríp,	no bráss in the gírdle;
But be shód with sándals,	and weár not two coáts.
When ye énter a hoúse,	ásk its wélfare,
And thére remaín	till ye gó thénce.
And thát which receíves you not,	nor heárs your wórd,
Sháke off its dúst	from óff your feét.
Lo I sénd you fórth	like sheép among wólves;
Be wíse as sérpents,	and hármless as dóves.'

Following upon this, *vv.* 17–22 are connected by the unrhythmical link 'But beware of men, for'. Then follows *v.* 23, peculiar to Matthew, of which at any rate the second half ('For verily I say unto you, ye shall not have gone through the cities of Israel, till the Son of Man be come') is evidently unrhythmical, and in this respect stands out of relation to its context—a striking fact when taken in connexion with the fact already noted (cf. foot-note, p. 121), that the introduction, *vv.* 5–7 (also peculiar to Matthew), which likewise limits the mission to Israel, is similarly unrhythmical. In the next section, however, *vv.* 24–27 (of which there is an abbreviation of *vv.* 24, 25 in Luke 6:40), four-beat rhythm is again unmistakable.

'The discíple is nót	abóve the máster,
And the sláve is nót	abóve his lórd.
Enoúgh to the discíple	that he bé as the máster,
And ⟨enoúgh⟩ to the sláve	⟨that he bé⟩ as his lórd.

If the máster of the hoúse	they have cálled Beelze-búl,
Hów much móre	the sóns of his hoúse.

Fear them not therefore, for

There is noúght conceáled	but shall bé reveáled,
And noúght that is híd	but shall cóme to be knówn.
What I téll you in dárkness,	speák in the líght,
And what ye heár in the eár	proclaím on the hoúse-tops.'

The rest of the chapter is uncharacterized by this form of rhythm.

The identity of rhythm in *vv.* $^{8-16}$, and *vv.* $^{17-22}$, $^{24-27}$, of Matt. 10 can scarcely, however, imply that they were originally parts of a single discourse. The first section is assigned by all three Synoptists to a temporary mission of the Twelve which took place during our Lord's ministry, and its contents suit such an occasion; *vv.* $^{17-22}$, on the other hand, clearly deal with the vicissitudes to be encountered by the Apostles in the longer future. The sections have simply been brought together by Matthew on account of the similarity of their contents.

Is, then, their identity of rhythm merely accidental? Looking at the other passages in which we have found illustrations of the use of four-beat rhythm, we can hardly fail to note that some of them certainly—the Lord's Prayer (cf. Luke 11^{1}), Luke $11^{9,10}$, $12^{32-37,42,43}$, Matt. 13^{52}, 16^{17-19}, and others at least primarily—Luke $6^{27-29,36-38}$, Matt. 6^{24},[1] are addressed to the inner

[1] The introductory words of Luke 6^{27}, 'Ἀλλ' ὑμῖν λέγω τοῖς ἀκούουσιν, may include an outer circle of listeners, but the instruction is intended primarily for the disciples (*v.* ^{20}).

circle of disciples and convey ethical teaching, and that in a calm and collected manner, untouched by strong emotion.[1] The remaining passage, Luke $7^{22, 23}$, falls into the same category as addressed to the disciples of John the Baptist. We have, in fact, in these passages examples of the ordinary method in which our Lord as a Rabbi instructed His followers, and it would seem that this four-beat rhythm was a form which He employed to convey such instruction. Now the two passages which we have been discussing, which both deal with the missionary work of the disciples, and which have been brought together in Matt. 10 on account of this common element in their contents, belong also to the same class of teaching; and that is the reason why both are cast in the characteristic four-beat rhythm.

We may add, as illustrative of the same form of rhythm, a passage from the Lucan account of the commission of the Seventy.

Luke 10^{16}.

'He that heáreth yoú, heáreth Mé;
And he that rejécteth yoú, rejécteth Mé;
And he that rejécteth Mé, rejécteth Him that sént Me.'

That our Lord was not alone in employing this rhythm in the instruction of disciples appears from the following passage from Hillel's teaching which is preserved in *Pirḳê Ābhôth* ii, 8. To illustrate the rhythm we give the passage first in the original Rabbinic Hebrew.

[1] This point is emphasized in view of the character of the discourses which are framed in the *Ḵīnā* rhythm. Cf. pp. 34 ff.

Marbé bāsā́r	*marbé rimmā́*
marbé n^{e}kāsī́m	*marbé d^{e}'āgā́*
marbé š^{e}phāḥṓth	*marbé zimmā́*
marbé '^{a}bādī́m	*marbé gāzḗl*
marbé nāšī́m	*marbé k^{e}šāphī́m*
marbé tōrā́	*marbé ḥayyī́m*
marbé ḥokmā́	*marbé y^{e}šībā́*
marbé ṣ^{e}dāḳā́	*marbé šālṓm*

'Who increáseth flésh,	increáseth wórms;
Who increáseth weálth,	increáseth cáre;
Who increáseth maíd-servants,	increáseth léwdness;
Who increáseth mén-servants,	increáseth théft;
Who increáseth wómen,	increáseth wítchcraft;
Who increáseth *Tṓrā*,	increáseth lífe;
Who increáseth wísdom,	increáseth schólars;
Who increáseth ríght-eousness,	increáseth peáce.'

The following sayings ascribed to early Rabbinic teachers in *Pirḳê Ābhôth* exhibit the same rhythm, and serve to indicate that it was an ordinary form in which such teaching was cast.

Simeon the Righteous (*op. cit.* i, 2).

'al š^{e}lōšā́ d^{e}bārī́m	*hā'ōlā́m 'ōmḗd*
'al hattōrā́ w^{e}'al hā'^{a}bōdā́	*w^{e}'al g^{e}mīlū́t ḥ^{a}sādī́m*
'On thrée concérns	the wórld is stáyed,
On the Láw and on the Sérvice	and on the récompense of kíndnesses.'

José ben-Joezer (*op. cit.* i, 4).

y^{e}hī́ bēt^{e}kā́	*bēt wā'ad lāḥ^{a}kāmī́m*
weh^{e}wḗ mit'abbḗḳ	*ba'^{a}phā́r raglēhḗm*
w^{e}šōtḗ b^{e}ṣim'ā́	*'et dibrēhḗm*

'Let thy hoúse becóme   a trýst for the wíse,
And be rólling thysélf   in the dúst of their feét,
And drínking with thírst   their weíghty wórds.'

Jose ben-Johanan (*op. cit.* i, 5).

y^{e}hī́ bēt^{e}kā́   *pātū́^{a}ḥ lār^{e}wāḥā́*
w^{e}yihyū́ '^{a}niyyī́m   *b^{e}nḗ bēt^{e}kā́*
w^{e}'al tarbḗ sīḥā́   *'im hā́'iššā́*

'Ópen thy hoúse   to its fúll extént,
And wélcome the poór   as sóns of thy hoúse,
And speák not at lárge   with wómenkínd.'

Joshua ben-Perachya (*op. cit.* i, 6).

'^{a}sḗ l^{e}kā ráb   *ūḳ^{e}nḗ l^{e}kā ḥābḗr*
weh^{e}wē dā́n 'et kol 'ādā́m   *l^{e}káph zākū́t*

'Máke thee a teácher   and gét thee a friénd,
And júdge every mán   by the scále of wórth.'

The Fourth Gospel does not contain a large amount of calm and measured instruction addressed to the inner circle of disciples, such as we find in the Synoptists. It does, however, contain the Last Discourses (*chs.* 14–16), which, if they represent a genuine tradition of our Lord's teaching, might well be expected to offer an echo of the characteristic rhythm ; and it is of great interest to notice that this seems clearly to be exhibited in the opening part of *ch.* 14.

1. 'Untroúbled be your heárts ;
Beliéve in Gód,   and beliéve in Mé.

2. In My Fáther's hoúse   are mány mánsions ;
Had it nót been só,   Í would have tóld you ;
For I gó to prepáre   for yoú a pláce.

3. And if I gó and prepáre   a pláce for yoú,

I will cóme agaín, and receíve you to Mysélf,
That whére Í am, ye toó may bé.

4. And whíther I gó ye knów the wáy.

5. Thomas saith to Him,
Lord, we know not whither Thou goest;
How can we know the way?

6. Jesus saith to him,
Í am the wáy and the trúth and the lífe;
None cómeth to the Fáther excépt through Mé.

7. If ye had récognized Mé, My Fáther ye would have knówn;
Hencefórth ye récognize Him and have loóked upón Him.

8. Philip saith to Him,
Lord, show us the Father, and it sufficeth us.

9. Jesus saith to him,
So lóng time wíth you, and thou hast not récognized Me, Phílip!
He that hath seén Mé, hath seén the Fáther;
Hów sayest thoú, Shów us the Fáther?'

10. Believest thou not that
Í am in the Fáther and the Fáther in Mé?
The wórds which I speák [unto you] I speák not of Mysélf,
But the Fáther abiding in Mé, Hé doeth His wórks.'

As much to convince himself as his readers that the detection of rhythm in this passage is not due to fancy, the present writer has translated it straightforwardly into Galilaean Aramaic; and he feels justified in claiming that the result bears out his conclusion.

1.	*lā yitbāhál libb^{e}kṓn*	
	hēmī́nū bēlāhā́	*ūbī́ hēmī́nū*
2.	*b^{e}bētḗh d^{e}'abbā́*	*m^{e}nāḥā́n saggī'ā́n*
	'īn lḗt hū́ k^{e}dḗn	*'^{a}marī́t l^{e}kṓn*
	d^{e}'āzēlnā́ d^{e}'atḳḗn	*'atár l^{e}kṓn*
3.	*w^{e}'īn 'ēzḗl w^{e}'atḳḗn*	*l^{e}kṓn 'atár*
	ṭūbā́n 'ātēnā́	*'^{a}ḳabb^{e}línn^{e}kōn lī́*
	d^{e}hā́n hāwēnā́	*'ūph 'attū́n t^{e}hṓn*
4.	*ūl^{e}hā́n 'āzēlnā́*	*yād'īttū́n 'ūrḥā́*
5.	*'āmar lēh T^{e}'ōmā*	
	mārān lēnan yād'īn l^{e}hān 'āzēlatt	
	hēk yād'īnān 'ūrḥā	
6.	*'āmar lēh Yēšūa'*	
	'^{a}nā hū́ 'urḥā́	*w^{e}ḳūšṭā́ w^{e}ḥayyḗ*
	lēt 'ātḗ l^{e}'abbā́	*'illūlḗ bīdī́*
7.	*'īn lī́ 'akkartū́n*	*'ūph l^{e}'abbā́ y^{e}da'tū́n*
	min kaddū́ 'akkartūnéh	*waḥ^{a}métūn léh*
8.	*'āmar lēh Philippos*	
	mārān 'awda' lan 'abbā ūmist^{e}yan	
9.	*'āmar lēh Yēšūa'*	
	zimnā dḗn 'amm^{e}kōn '^{a}nā́ w^{e}lā 'akkartánī Phílippè	
	man d^{e}ḥā́mē lī́	*ḥ^{a}mā́ l^{e}'abbā́*
	hḗk 'att 'āmár	*'awda' lā́n 'abbā́*
10.	*lēt m^{e}hēmīnatt*	
	da'^{a}nā́ be'abbā́	*w^{e}'abbā́ hū bī́*
	millayyā́ dim^{e}mallēlnā́ [lekōn]	*lā m^{e}mallēlnā́ min garmī́*
	'abbā́ dim^{e}kattar bī́	*hū 'ābḗd 'ōbādṓy*

If our conclusion is well grounded that this passage really offers an example of the four-beat rhythm which we have seen to characterize similar teaching in the Synoptists, we have here a fact which is of the first importance for the substantial authenticity of the Last Discourses. Without maintaining that they represent throughout the *ipsissima verba* of our Lord, we may reasonably infer that they have been recorded by an actual hearer, in whose mind the familiar rhythm was still running, even after a long lapse of years, and who was able to record with substantial accuracy the well-remembered words in the form in which they were conveyed. It does not of course follow that, in order to prove the authenticity of the rest of the Discourses, they must be shown to be in the same rhythm throughout. The Synoptic evidence rather suggests that our Lord varied the form in which He conveyed His teaching to His disciples. Traces of the same rhythm can, however, be detected elsewhere in the Discourses; cf. $14^{15, 18, 21\,a, 23\,a, 24\,a, 27}$, 15^{5}.

Examples of four-beat rhythm in other passages in the Fourth Gospel are the following:

John 3^{18}.

'He that beliéveth on Hím   is nót condémned;
He that beliéveth nót   is alreády condémned.

John $3^{20, 21}$.

'Whoso dóeth íll   háteth the líght,
And cómeth not to the líght   lest his wórks should be condémned;
But he that wórketh the trúth   cómeth to the líght,
That his deéds may be mánifest   that they are wroúght in Gód.'

John 6[35, 37].

'He that cómeth to Mé	shall néver húnger,
And he that beliéveth on Mé	shall néver thírst.
. . .	. . .
All that the Fáther gíveth Me	shall cóme to Mé,
And him that cómeth to Mé	I will in nó wise cast oút.'

Three-beat rhythm.

This is fairly frequent in the Synoptic Gospels, and seems mainly to characterize pithy sayings of a gnomic character, akin to the proverbs of the Old Testament, such as are found in the Sermon on the Mount. Three-beat rhythm is the rhythm of the Beatitudes (Matt. 5[3ff.]). Cf. the Aramaic rendering given on p. 166. Other examples are the following:

Matt. 5[14–16] (no parallel).

'Yé are the líght of the wórld.
A cíty cannót be híd,
Which is sét on the tóp of a híll.
Neíther líght they a lámp,
And sét it beneáth a búshel;
Bút on the lámp-stand ⟨they sét it⟩,
And it líghteth all thóse in the hoúse.
So shíne your líght before mén,
That they may seé your wórks that are goód,
And may glórify your fáther who is in heáven.'[1]

Rendered into Aramaic this would run:

'attū́n n^{e}hōrḗh d^{e}ʿāl^{e}mā́
lā yāk^{e}lā́ m^{e}dīnā́ d^{e}tiṭṭamár

[1] For the words supplied in brackets, cf. Syr. Sin.

dîl'ēl min ṭûr mittᵉsāmâ
wᵉlâ madlᵉḳîn bōṣīnâ
ūmᵉsīmîn tᵉḥôt mōdᵉyâ
'ellâ 'al mᵉnortâ ⟨mᵉsīmīn lēh⟩
wᵉhū manhâr lᵉkullᵉhôn dibᵉbētâ
hēkdēn yanhâr nᵉhōrᵉkôn ḳᵉdām bᵉnē 'ᵉnāšâ
dᵉyiḥmôn 'ōbādēkôn šappīrîn
wīšabbᵉḥûn la'ᵃbūkôn dᵉbišmayyâ

Matt. $6^{22,23}$ = Luke $11^{34,35}$.

'The líght of the bódy is the éye.
If so bé thine éye be síngle,
Áll thy bódy is líght;
But if so bé thine éye be évil,
Áll thy bódy is dárk;
And if the líght that is ín thee be dárk,
Thén the dárkness how greát!'[1]

bōṣīnēh dᵉpigrâ hī 'ēnâ
'īn hāwᵉyâ 'ēnâk pᵉšīṭâ
kullēh pigrâk nᵉhîr
wᵉ'īn hāwᵉyâ 'ēnâk bīšâ
kullēh pigrâk ḳᵉbîl
wᵉ'īn nᵉhōrâ dᵉbâk ḳᵉbîl
hû ḳablâ ḥad kᵉmâ

Matt. 7^{6} (no parallel).

'Do not gíve that which is hóly to the dógs,
Neither cást ye your peárls before swíne;
Lest they trample them with their feet,
And turn and rend you.'

[1] The text adopted is that of Matthew, which is rhythmically superior to Luke's. Luke 11^{36}, which continues the same theme, does not in its present form exhibit any trace of rhythm.

The second couplet appears in English to consist of two-beat stichoi; but that the rhythm is properly the same as that of the first couplet appears from the Aramaic rendering.

lā tīhᵃbū́n ḳudšā́ lᵉkalbayyā́
wᵉlā tirmū́n margālyātkṓn ḳᵉdām ḥᵃzīrayyā́
dᵉlā yᵉdū́šūn 'innṓn bᵉraglēhṓn
wītū́būn wībázzᵉ'ūnkṓn

Matt. 8[20] = Luke 9[58].

'To the fóxes thére are hóles,
To the bírds of the heáven nésts;
But to the Són of Mán there is nót
Whére He may láy His heád.'[1]

lᵉta'layyā́ 'īt lᵉhṓn bōrī́n
lᵉ'ōphā́ dišmayyā́ ḳinnī́n
ūlᵉbár 'ᵉnāšā́ lēt lḗh
hā́n dᵉyarkḗn rēšḗh

Luke 9[62] (no parallel).

'Whoso pútteth his hánd to the ploúgh,
And túrneth his gáze to the reár,
Is not fít for the kíngdom of Gód.'

man dᵉrāmḗ yᵉdḗh 'al paddānā́
ūmístakkál la'ᵃḥōrā́
lēt šāwḗ lᵉmalkūtḗh dēlāhā́

Matt. 12[30] = Luke 11[23].

'Hé that is not wíth Me is agaínst Me,
And he that gáthereth not wíth Me, scáttereth.'[1]

man dᵉlēt hū́ 'immī́ lᵉḳiblī́
ūdᵉlā kānḗš 'immī́ mᵉbaddár

[1] The two versions are identical.

Matt. 15^{14} = Luke 6^{39}.

'If the blínd leád the blínd,
Bóth shall fáll into the dítch.'[1]

'īn yidbár samyā́ lᵉsamyā́
tᵉrēhṓn nāphᵉlī́n bᵉgumṣā́

The following passage of a different type is cast in the same rhythm.

Matt. 11^{25-27} = Luke $10^{21,22}$.

'I give thánks unto Theé, O Fáther,
Thou Lórd of heáven and éarth,
Because Thou hast hid these thíngs from the wíse [and prúdent],
And hast reveálèd thém to bábes;
Yea, Fáther, ⟨I gíve Thee glóry⟩,
For só it seemed goód in Thy síght.

Áll things are delívered to Me by My Fáther;
And none knóweth the Són save the Fáther;
Neither knóweth any the Fáther save the Són,
And hé to whom the Són will reveál Him.'

An Aramaic rendering of this passage is given on p. 171.

Examples of the use of three-beat rhythm are fairly frequent in the Fourth Gospel.

John 3^{11}.

'Thát which we knów we speák,
And thát which we have seén we téstify;
And our téstimony ye are nót receíving.'

mā́ dᵉyādᵉʿīnā́n mᵉmallᵉlīnā́n
ūmā́ daḥᵃmḗnan mashᵃdīnā́n
wᵉsahᵃdūtā́n lēt 'attū́n nāsᵉbī́n

[1] Cast in an interrogative form in Luke. The difference is due to the fact that אִין, 'if', may also introduce a question.

John 4^{36}.

'He that reápeth receíveth wáges,
And gáthereth fruít unto lífe [eternal].'

man d^e ḥāṣḗd 'agrā́ nāsḗb
ūm^e kannḗš pērī́n l^e ḥayyī́n

John 6^{35}.

'Í am the breád of lífe;
He that cómeth to Mé shall not húnger,
And he that beliéveth shall not thírst for éver.'

'^a nā hū́ laḥmā́ d^e ḥayyī́n
man d^e 'ātḗ l^e wātī́ lā kāphḗn
ūman dimhēmīn bī́ lā ṣāḥḗ l^e 'ālám

John 6^{55}.

'My flésh is meát indeéd,
And My bloód is drínk indeéd.'

bisrī́ min ḳ^e šṓṭ mēkā́l
w^e 'idmī́ min ḳ^e šṓṭ mištḗ[1]

John 6^{63}.

'The spírit it ís that quíckeneth,
The flésh prófiteth nóthing;
The thíngs of which I spáke unto yoú,
Spírit are théy and lífe.'

rūḥā́ hī hādā́ d^e maḥyā́
bisrā́ ḳ^e lū́m lā mah^a nḗ
millayyā́ d^e mall^e lḗt l^e kṓn
rū^a ḥ 'innū́n w^e ḥayyī́n

John 8^{12}.

'Í am the líght of the wórld;
He that fólloweth Me shall not wálk in dárkness,
But shall háve the líght of lífe.'

[1] Or according to the variant reading, 'true bread . . . true drink', *mēkā́l ḳaššīṭ . . . mištḗ ḳaššīṭ.*

'ᵃnā hū́ nᵉhōrēh dᵉ'ālᵉmā́
man dᵉdābēḳ lī lā mᵉhallḗk bᵉḳablā́
'ellā hāwē lēh nᵉhōrā́ dᵉḥayyī́n

John 8[31, 32].

'If yé abíde in My wórd,
Of a trúth My discíples are yé;
And ye shall knów the trúth,
And the trúth shall máke you freé.'

'īn 'attū́n mᵉkattᵉrī́n bᵉmilláy
min ḳᵉšōṭ talmīdáy 'attū́n
wᵉtakkᵉrū́n leh lᵉḳūšṭā́
wᵉḳūšṭā́ ḥārḗr lᵉkṓn

Here the third line appears to exhibit two beats only.

John 8[34-36].

'Éveryone that wórketh sín,
The sláve of sín is hé.
The sláve abídeth not in the hoúse [for éver];
The són abídeth for éver.
If the són máke you freé,
Trúly freé shall ye bé.'

kol mán dᵉ'ābḗd ḥeṭ'ā́
'abdḗh dᵉḥeṭ'ā́ īt hū́
'abdā́ lā mᵉkattár bᵉbētā́ [lᵉ'ālám]
bᵉrā́ mᵉkattár lᵉ'ālám
'īn bᵉrā́ ḥārḗr. lᵉkṓn
min ḳᵉšōṭ bᵉnē ḥōrī́n 'attū́n

John 8[39].

'If chíldren of Ábraham ye áre,
The wórks of Ábraham ye dó.'

'īn b^{e}nṓhī d^{e}'Abrāhā́m hāwēttū́n
'^{a}bādṓhī d^{e}'Abrāhā́m 'āb^{e}dīttū́n[1]

John 13^{16}.

'A sérvant is not greáter than his lórd,
Nor a méssenger than hím that sént him.'

lēt '^{a}bḗd ráb min mārḗh
ūš^{e}lī́aḥ min hāhū́ d^{e}šalḥḗh

It is noticeable that some of the examples characterized by this rhythm (John 4^{36}, 6^{63a}, 8^{34-36}, 13^{16}) are of the nature of aphorisms, resembling in this respect examples in the same rhythm cited from the Synoptic Gospels.

Other instances from the Fourth Gospel of three-beat rhythm are $6^{26,27}$, and (in the main) 10^{1-5}; Aramaic renderings of these passages will be found on pp. 170, 174.

A few examples of this rhythm are to be found in *Pirḳê Ābhôth.* Thus we have the opening saying ascribed to 'the men of the Great Synagogue' who were the traditional successors of Ezra (*op. cit.* I. 1).

h^{e}yū́ m^{e}tūnī́m baddī́n
w^{e}ha'^{a}mī́du talmīdī́m harbḗ
wa'^{a}sū s^{e}yā́g lattōrā́

[1] Here *hāwēttūn*, *'āb^{e}dīttūn* are participles combined with the 2nd pl. pers. pronoun, lit. 'ye being', 'ye doing'; and since the participle denotes mere *duration*, apart from mark of time, the sense implied might equally well be, 'ye were being . . . ye would be doing' (or, 'ye would have been doing'). The sense adopted above conforms to the better-attested Greek reading ἔστε . . . ποιεῖτε, but the same Aramaic would yield the sense of the other current reading ἦτε . . . ἐποιεῖτε (ἄν), which is probably a correction dictated by a sense of greater fitness to the context.

'Bé delíberate in júdgement,
And raíse up discíples full mány,
And máke a hédge to the Láw.'

Hillel (i. 14).

'im 'ḗn 'ᵃnī lī́ mī lī́
ūkᵉšeʾᵃnī́ lᵉʿaṣmī́ mā lī́
weʾim lṓ ʿakšā́w 'ēmātáy

'If nót for mysélf, who is fór me?
And íf for mysẹ́lf, who ám I?
And íf not nów, pray whén?'

Ḳīnā-rhythm.

Is it possible to trace, among the utterances of our Lord, any passages which seem to exhibit the characteristic rhythm of the Hebrew *Ḳīnā* or dirge—a rhythm which, as we have seen (pp. 34, 39), was by no means confined to this particular form of poem, but was used more widely in poetry of an emotional type? In the examples which are now to be given it is at any rate a striking fact that all are found among passages marked by strong emotion—moving the deepest human feelings of the Speaker, and calculated to react in the same way upon His hearers. The first example which we shall take belongs to Q, and is found in Luke 13^{23-27} (partial parallels, not similarly rhythmical, in Matt. $7^{13,22,23}$). It will be noticed that in this passage the whole is not rhythmical, as a carefully elaborated poem would be, but there is a setting which structurally takes the form of prose, yet which by no means detracts from the solemn and mournful flow of the *Ḳīnā*-verses. In the rendering which we give these latter are distinguished by indentation and stress-accents.

23. 'And one said to Him, Lord, are there few that
shall be saved? And He said to them,

24. Exért yoursélves to énter
by the nárrow gáte;
For mány [I say unto you] shall seék to énter,
and shall nót be áble.

25. Once the máster of the hoúse hath arísen,
and hath shút the doór,
And ye begín to stánd withoút,
and to knóck the doór,
saying, Lord, open to us;
and He shall answer and say to you,
Í have no knówledge óf you,
whénce ye áre;

26. then shall ye begin to say;
We did éat and drínk befóre Thee,
and Thou didst téach in our streéts;

27. and He shall say, I say unto you,
Í have no knówledge óf you,
whénce ye áre;
Gét you awáy from Mé,
all ye wórkers of iníquity.'

In order to show how perfectly this represents the Hebrew *Ḳīnā*, we give a Hebrew rendering in Biblical style.

24. *hítkatt^{e}šū́ lābṓ*
baššá'ar haṣṣā́r
kī rabbī́m y^{e}baḳḳ^{e}šū́ lābṓ
w^{e}lṓ yūkā́lū

25. *'im ḳā́m bá'al habbáyit*
wayyisgṓr haddélet
w^{e}tāḥḗllū la'^{a}mṓd baḥū́ṣ
w^{e}lidpṓḳ 'al haddélet

lēmōr '^{a}dōnāy pitḥā lānū
w^{e}'ānā w^{e}'āmar '^{a}lēkem
'ēnénnī yōdḗ^{a}' 'etkém
mē'áyin 'attém

26. *'āz tāḥēllū l^{e}dabbēr*
'ākálnu w^{e}šātī́nū l^{e}phānékā
ūb^{e}šūḳḗnū limmā́dtā

27. *w^{e}'āmar 'āmartī lākem*
'ēnénnī yōdḗ^{a}' 'etkém
mē'áyin 'attém
sū́rū lakém mimménnī
kol pṓ'^{a}lē 'ā́wen

If we now translate the passage into Galilaean Aramaic, the *Ḳīnā*-rhythm is no less clear.

24. *'ítkatt^{e}šū́n l^{e}mē'ál*
b^{e}tar'ā́ 'āy^{e}ḳā́
d^{e}saggī'ī́n yib'ṓn l^{e}mē'ál
w^{e}lā́ yāk^{e}lī́n

25. *kad ḳā́m mārḗh d^{e}baytā́*
wa'^{a}ḥád dāšā́
ūt^{e}šārṓn ḳāy^{e}mī́n b^{e}bārā́
ūmaḳḳ^{e}šī́n 'al dāšā́
w^{e}'ām^{e}rīn māran p^{e}taḥ lan
w^{e}hū 'ānē w^{e}'āmar l^{e}kōn
lēnā́ makkḗr l^{e}kṓn
min hā́n 'attū́n

26. *b^{e}kēn t^{e}šārōn 'ām^{e}rīn*
'^{a}kálnan ūš^{e}tī́nan ḳ^{o}dāmā́k
ūb^{e}šūḳēnan 'allḗpht

27. *w^{e}hū 'āmar 'āmarnā l^{e}kōn*
lēnā́ makkḗr l^{e}kṓn
min hā́n 'attū́n

'itraḥᵃḳūn minnī
kol 'ābᵉdē šiḳrā [1]

The following fairly lengthy passages from Mark appear to be framed in this rhythm.

Mark 2^{19-22} = Matt. 9^{15-17} = Luke 5^{34-39}.

'Can the chíldren of the bríde-chamber moúrn
while the brídegroom is wíth them?
So lóng as the brídegroom is wíth them
they cánnot fást.
But the dáys shall cóme when the brídegroom shall be táken fróm them,
and thén shall they fást.
No one pútteth a pátch of néw clóth
upon an óld gárment;
For its fúlness táketh from the gárment,
and a [worse] rént is máde.
Neither poúr they néw wíne
into óld wíne-skins;
Ótherwise the wíne-skins are rént,
and the wíne is spílled [and the skins perish].
But [they put] néw wíne into frésh wíne-skins,
and bóth are presérved.' [2]

[1] In the Hebrew and Aramaic renderings it is assumed that ἀφ' οὗ in *v.* [25] represents an original 'When', introducing a new sentence after a full stop. The apodosis is then most naturally to be found in 'and (= then) ye shall begin to stand without' (i.e. καὶ ἄρξεσθε in place of καὶ ἄρξησθε); though it is possible to treat this as a continuation of the protasis, and to find the apodosis in 'and (= then) he shall answer, &c.' It seems clear, however, that Luke, in rendering ἀφ' οὗ . . . καὶ ἄρξησθε, intended a close connexion with the preceding sentence—'shall not be able, from the time when, &c.'

[2] Here we follow the text of Matthew, which, as judged by the rhythmical standard, is certainly superior to that of Mark. Note that in Mark 2^{19} the placing of the infinitive νηστεύειν after the temporal clause (so Luke ποιῆσαι νηστεύειν) is less natural in a Semitic language

Mark 8^{34-38} = Matt. 16^{24-27} = Luke 9^{23-26}.

'If any wísheth to cóme after Mé,
    let him denÿ himsélf;
And let him táke up his cróss daíly,
    and cóme after Mé.

For whoso wísheth to sáve his lífe,
    hé shall lóse it;
But whoso lóseth his lífe for My sáke,
    hé shall sáve it.

For what prófiteth a mán if he gáin the whole wórld,
    and fórfeit his lífe?
Or whát shall a mán gíve
    in excháage for his lífe?

than is the position of πενθεῖν in Matthew after the verb which governs it and before the temporal clause. In Mark 2^{20} the addition of ἐν ἐκείνῃ τῇ ἡμέρᾳ (Luke ἐν ἐκείναις ταῖς ἡμέραις) throws out the rhythm by adding two stresses to the short two-stress member of the *Ḳīnā*-verse, and is not found in Matthew. In Matt. 9^{16} οὐδεὶς δὲ ἐπιβάλλει ἐπίβλημα ῥάκους ἀγνάφου κτλ. gives the original Semitic order of words rather than Mark 2^{21}, οὐδεὶς ἐπίβλημα ῥάκους ἀγνάφου ἐπιρράπτει κτλ. In Mark 2^{21} εἰ δὲ μή, αἴρει τὸ πλήρωμα ἀπ' αὐτοῦ τὸ καινὸν τοῦ παλαιοῦ is more awkward than Matthew's simple and rhythmical αἴρει γὰρ τὸ πλήρωμα αὐτοῦ ἀπὸ τοῦ ἱματίου, and has the air of an unnecessary attempt at explanation (Luke's parallel is clearly paraphrastic). May we not infer from these facts that the passage really belonged originally to Q, and was derived thence by Mark less faithfully than by Matthew? The only passage given above which is not found in Matthew is the second *Ḳīnā*-verse, derived from Mark 2^{19b}, which is adopted as perfectly rhythmical and as possibly omitted through accident by Matthew owing to its resemblance to the temporal clause in the preceding question. It is possible, however, that both this and the last verse ('But they put new wine, &c.'), which is not found in Mark, may be of the nature of explanatory additions; in which case we would have three couplets, dealing respectively with the children of the bridechamber, the garment, and the new wine. The words in square brackets are so marked as rhythmically superfluous. In regard to the last, we may note that 'New wine into fresh skins' may very likely have been a current proverbial saying.

For the Son of Mán shall cóme in the glóry of His
Fáther
with His hóly ángels,
And thén shall He rénder to eách
accórding to his wórk.'[1]

On the occurrence of more than three stresses in the first member of the *Ḳīnā*-verse, as occurs a few times in each of these passages, cf. p. 42.

In the parable of the Sheep and the Goats (Matt. 25[31 ff.]) it is very striking that, when the emotion reaches its highest point, the rhythm at once becomes that of the *Ḳīnā* (*vv.* [34 ff.]).

'Then the king shall say to those on his right hand,
Cóme, ye bléssed of my Fáther,
Inhérit the kíngdom prepáred for you
from the foundátion of the wórld.
Becaúse I was húngry and ye féd me;
I was thírsty, and ye refréshed me.

[1] Here again, if our rhythmical scheme is right, Matthew represents the nearest approximation to the original; and the version given above presents this text, except that in the second *Ḳīnā*-verse we have adopted καθ' ἡμέραν from Luke, and in the fourth verse Luke's οὗτος as representing an emphatic הוּא, which we assume to have stood also in the corresponding clause in the third verse. We assume also in the fourth verse that Mark and Luke σώσει, which gives a complete inversion of terms ('save . . . lose', 'lose . . . save') is original rather than Matthew εὑρήσει (cf. p. 74). The fact that the addition καὶ τοῦ εὐαγγελίου in Mark 8[35] spoils the characteristic form of our Lord's antithetic parallelism, and is therefore probably a gloss, has already been noted (cf. p. 74). Finally, the last two *Ḳīnā*-verses, as they stand in Matt. 16[27], are perfect in form if we adopt 'holy' before 'angels' from Mark and Luke (so D, Pesh. in Matt.), but the corresponding passage in Mark 8[38], Luke 9[26], seems to show no trace of *Ḳīnā*- or other form of rhythm. It would seem to follow that this also is originally a Q passage, which Matthew has preserved more accurately in the main than Mark.

A stránger was Í, and ye hoúsed me;
náked, and ye clád me.
Síck was Í, and ye vísited me;
in príson, and ye cáme unto me.

Then shall the righteous answer him, saying,
Lord,
When sáw we thee húngry and noúrished thee;
or thírsty and refréshed thee?
When sáw we thee a stránger and hoúsed thee,
or náked, and clád thee?
When sáw we thee síck, ⟨and vísited thee⟩;
or in príson, and cáme unto thee?

And the king shall answer and say unto them,
Vérily I sáy unto yoú,
Thát which ye díd unto óne of these léast of my bréthren,
unto mé ye díd it.'[1]

An Aramaic rendering of the first half of the parable is given on p. 172.

[1] In *v.* [36], *ἠσθένησα καὶ ἐπεσκέψασθέ με, ἐν φυλακῇ ἤμην καὶ ἤλθατε πρός με*, the supposition of a word-for-word translation would give two stresses only to the first half-verse, and three to the second: 'I was sick, and ye vísited me; | in príson was Í, and ye cáme unto me'; and so Pal. Syr. ܐܬܒܝܫܬ ܘܣܥܪܬܘܢܝ ܗܘܝܬ .·. ܒܚܒܘܫܝܐ ܗܘܝܬ ܘܐܬܝܬܘܢ ܠܘܬܝ., i. e. *ἠσθένησα* is represented by a single verbal form *'etbīšet*, and *ἤμην* has its equivalent in the substantive verb *h^a^wīt*. The rendering which we presuppose is מְרַע הֲוֵית וְאַסְעֲרְתּוּנִי | בַּחֲבוּשְׁיָא וְאַלְוֵיתוּנִי, i.e. *m^e^ra' h^a^wēt* = lit. *ἀσθενὴς ἤμην*; and *ἤμην* in the second half-verse is understood and not expressed. This gives us our 3 + 2 stress *Ḳīnā*-verse, and may be held to be justified in view of the clear indications that the passage as a whole is cast in this rhythm. The addition in angular brackets in *v.* [39] is supplied from *v.*[36], as parallelism and rhythm demand.

The Fourth Gospel supplies one striking example of this rhythm.

John 16^{20-22}.

'*Yé* shall wéep and lamént,
but the wórld shall rejóice;
Yé shall be sórrowful, but your sórrow
shall be túrned into jóy.

A wóman when she is in trávail hath sórrow,
because her hoúr is cóme;
But whén she is delívered of the chíld,
she remémbereth not the ánguish
[for joy that a man is born into the world].

And yé also nów have sórrow,
but I will sée you agáin,
And your héart shall rejoíce, and your jóy
none táketh fróm you.'

The passage in square brackets, which breaks the rhythm, may well be an explanatory addition to the original words. In the second and last *Ḳīnā*-verses the caesura is purely formal, the sense-division giving 2 + 3 stresses. This can be paralleled from the Old Testament: cf. the examples given on p. 39.

Shorter passages in the Synoptists in the same rhythm are the following:

Matt. 11^{28-30} (no parallel).

'Cóme unto Mé, all ye weáry and búrdened,
and Í will refrésh you.
Táke My yóke upón you,
and leárn of Mé;

For meék am Í and lówly of heárt,
        and ye shall rést your soúls.
For My yóke is eásy,
        and My búrden líght'.[1]

Matt. $13^{16,17}$ = Luke $10^{23,24}$.

'Bléssed are your éyes, for they sée,
        and your éars, for they heár.
Verily I say unto you,
Mány próphets and ríghteous have desíred to sée
  the thíngs which ye sée,
        and have nót seén,
And to heár the things which ye heár,
        and have nót heárd.'[2]

Luke $10^{41,42}$ (no parallel).

'Martha, Martha,
  Thou art cáreful and troúbled about mány things;
        but óne thing is neédful;
  And Máry hath chósen the goód part,
        which shall not be táken fróm her.'

In *v.* [28] *ἀναπαύσω ὑμᾶς* represents a single term in the original, viz. the Aph'el (causative) form of *nūᵃḥ*, 'to rest', with pronominal suffix, *'ᵃnīḥᵃkôn*, which, with the emphatic personal pronoun *'ᵃnā́* preceding, gives the two stresses of the second member of the verse—hence the rendering 'and Í will refrésh you' rather than the familiar 'and I will give you rest', which suggests three stresses. It is assumed that in *v.* [29] *καὶ εὑρήσετε ἀνάπαυσιν* likewise represents the Aph'el of this verb, *ūtᵉnīḥūn*.

[2] דְּחָזְיָן . . . דְּשָׁמְעִין may mean either 'because they see . . . because they hear' (Matt. *ὅτι βλέπουσιν . . . ὅτι ἀκούουσιν*), or 'which see . . . which hear' (Luke *οἱ βλέποντες*). On the ambiguity of the demonstrative particle דְּ as leading at times to mistranslation (*ὅτι* for relative, and *vice versa*) cf. the writer's *Aramaic Origin of the Fourth Gospel*, pp. 76 ff.

In Matt. 23^{37-39} = Luke $13^{34, 35}$ we have our Lord's lament over Jerusalem, which might be expected to be cast into the form of a *Ḳīnā*; and this seems to be so.

'Jerúsalem, Jerúsalem, that sláyeth the próphets,
        and stóneth her méssengers,
How mány tímes have I lónged
        to gáther thy chíldren,
Like a hén that gáthereth her chícks
        beneáth her wíngs:
Yet ye would not.
Behóld, there remaíneth to yoú
        your hoúse a desolátion.
I say unto you, ye shall not see Me until ye say,
    Bléssed He that cómeth in the náme of the
        Lórd.'[1]

Here *καὶ οὐκ ἠθελήσατε* falls like a sigh between the second and third *Ḳīnā*-verses. The last line—a quotation from Ps. 118^{26}—has four stresses in Hebrew:

bārū́k habbā́ bešḗm Yahwéh.

[1] Matthew and Luke are nearly identical; but Matthew gives ἐπισυνάγει after ὄρνις, while Luke leaves it to be inferred from the preceding ἐπισυνάξαι (Matt. ἐπισυναγαγεῖν), and Matthew's ἔρημος is omitted by Luke. Both these words are essential to the rhythm, and Matthew may therefore be considered to offer a closer reproduction of the original Aramaic than Luke.

IV

THE USE OF RHYME BY OUR LORD

TRANSLATION into Aramaic of the portions of our Lord's teaching which exhibit the characteristics of Hebrew poetry reveals a further interesting fact, namely, that He seems not infrequently to have made use of *Rhyme*. This is the more remarkable in view of the infrequency of this trait in the literary poetry of the Old Testament, in which the few occurrences which can be collected seem for the most part to be rather accidental than designed, and opportunities for rhyming offered by the use of similar suffix-forms in parallel expressions are neglected, if not avoided. For example, Ps. 2 contains rhymes in *v.* [3] *mōsᵉrōtḗmō* 'their bonds', *ʿᵃbōtḗmō* 'their cords'; *v.* [6] *malkī́* 'my king', *har ḳodšī́* 'my holy hill' ('hill of my holiness'). Had the poet, however, been set upon rhyming, he might have produced it in *v.* [5] by rhyming *bᵉʾappṓ* 'in his anger' with *baḥᵃrōnṓ* 'in his hot displeasure'; or *ʾēlḗmō* 'unto them' with *yᵉbahᵃlḗmō* 'he shall dismay them'. Instead of this, he deliberately prefers the literary elegance of contrasted position of the parallel verbs—first in the sentence in stichos *a*, but last in stichos *b*:

ʾāz yᵉdabbḗr ʾēlḗmō bᵉʾappṓ
ūbáḥᵃrōnṓ yᵉbahᵃlḗmō

'Then shall He spéak unto thém in His ánger,
And in His hót displeásure He shall dismáy them.'

Similarly, in *v.* [8] *naḥ^a^lātékā* 'thine inheritance' is not rhymed with *'^a^ḥuzzātékā* 'thy possession', nor in *v.* [9] is *t^e^rō'ém* 'thou shalt break them' rhymed with *t^e^napp^e^ṣém* 'thou shalt shatter them', but the device of contrasted position is adopted as in *v.* [5]. In Ps. 54 we find three examples of rhyme (*vv.* [3,4,6] Heb.; *vv.* [1,2,4] E.VV.); but this is exceptional.

There is, however, a class of ancient Hebrew poetry in which the use of rhyme was probably a favourite device, namely, the popular poetry of the relatively uncultured. Not much of this has survived in the Old Testament; but, considering its paucity, it is remarkable how frequently it is characterized by the obviously intentional use of rhyme. An instance, in the crudest doggerel form, is seen in the song which is ascribed to the Philistine populace upon the captivity of Samson, Judges 16[24].

nātán 'elōhḗnū
b^e^yādḗnū 'et 'ōy^e^bḗnū
w^e'^et maḥ^a^ríb 'arṣḗnū
wa'^a^šer hirbā́ 'et ḥ^a^lālḗnū

'Our gód has gíven
Into our hánd our énemy,
And him who rávaged our lánd,
And múltiplied our slaín.'

Here the rhyme is formed by the suffix *-ḗnū* 'our' in conjunction with the varying radical preceding. Another instance from the Samson stories is seen in Judges 14[18], with rhyme on the suffix *-í* 'my'.

lūlḗ ḥ^a^raštém b^e'^eglātí
lṓ m^e^ṣātém ḥīdātí

'Hád ye not plówed with my heífer,
Ye hád not discóvered my ríddle.'

Similar in character is the improvisation of the women who greet Saul and David after the victory over the Philistines, 1 Sam. 18^7 (rhyme on *-āw* 'his').

hikkā́ Šā'ū́l ba'ᵃlāphā́w
wᵉDāwī́d bᵉríbᵉbōtā́w

'Saúl has slaín his thoúsands,
And Dávid his téns of thoúsands.'

The ancient 'Song of the Sword', Gen. $4^{23,24}$ (the English rendering of which has been given on pp. 30, 31), offers a rhyme upon the suffix *-ī* 'my' which is clearly not accidental.

'Ādā́ wᵉṢillā́ šᵉmá'an ḳōlī́
nᵉšē Lémek ha'ᵃzḗnnā 'imrātī́
kī 'ī́š hārágtī lᵉphiṣ'ī́
wᵉyéled lᵉḥabbū́rātī́
kī́ šib'ātáyim yuḳḳam Ḳáyin
wᵉLémek šib'ī́m wᵉšib'ā́

In Isaac's blessing of Jacob in Gen. 27 we find two rhyming couplets in *v.* ^{29}.

yá'abdū́kā 'ammī́m
wᵉyištaḥᵃwū́ lᵉkā́ lᵉ'ummī́m
hᵉwḗ gᵉbī́r lᵉ'aḥḥékā
wᵉyištaḥᵃwū́ lᵉkā́ bᵉnē 'imměkā

'Sérvice be dóne thee by peóples,
Hómage paíd thee by nátions;
Bé thou lórd o'er thy bréthren,
Yield thee hómage the sóns of thy móther.'

In the first couplet the rhyme is formed by the plural termination *-ī́m*; in the second by the suffix *-ékā* 'thy'.

Jacob's blessing of Judah (Gen. 49^{11}) yields a quatrain rhymed throughout on the suffix *-ṓ* 'his'.

'ōsᵉrī́ laggéphen 'īrṓ
wᵉlassōrḗḳā bᵉnī́ 'atōnṓ
kibbḗs bayyáyin lᵉbūšṓ
ūbᵉdám 'ᵃnābī́m sūtṓ

'Bínding to the víne his foál,
And to the choíce vine the cólt of his áss,
He hath wáshed in wíne his gárment,
And in the bloód of grápes his raíment.'

In the old poem on Sihon king of the Amorites in Num. 21 we have, in *v.* [28], an example of a quatrain with rhyming stichoi 1, 2, and 4, and non-rhyming 3, as so frequently in Arabic poetry.

kī 'ḗš yāṣᵉ'ā́ mē Ḥešbṓn
lehābā́ miḳḳiryát Sīḥṓn
'ā́kᵉlā 'Ár Mō'ā́b
bā'ᵃrā́ bāmṓt 'Arnṓn [1]

'For fíre went fórth from Heshbón,
A fláme from the tówn of Sihón;
It devoúred Ár of Moáb,
It kíndled the heíghts of Arnón.'

Precisely similar is Balaam's oracle against the Kenites in Num. $24^{21,22}$.

'ḗtān mṓšabékā
wᵉsī́m bᵉséla' ḳinnékā
kī 'im yihyé lᵉbā́'ēr Ḳáyin
'ad mā́ 'Aššū́r tišbékā

[1] Emending בָּעֲרָה, 'It kindled', in place of בַּעֲלֵי, 'The lords of', as demanded by the context.

'Endúring ís thy dwélling,
And sét in the crág thy nést;
Yet déstined for wásting is Ḳáyin,
Till Ásshur cárry thee cáptive.'

The most frequent use of rhyme in the Old Testament is found in the Song of Songs, which is undoubtedly based upon popular folk-song. This has been illustrated by the present writer in *Journal of Theological Studies*, x (July 1909), pp. 584 ff. An instance of an elaborately rhymed poem may be seen in *ch.* 8^{1-3}.

mí yittenkā́ kᵉ'āḥ lī́
yōnḗḳ šᵉdḗ 'immī́
'emṣā'ᵃkā́ baḥū́ṣ 'eššāḳᵉkā́
gám lō yābū́zū lī́
'enhāgᵉkā́ 'ᵃbī'ᵃkā́
'el bḗt 'immī́ tᵉlammᵉdḗnī
'ašḳᵉkā́ miyyḗn hārḗḳaḥ
mḗ'ᵃsī́s rimmōnī́
sᵉmṓlō táḥat rōšī́
wī́mīnṓ tᵉḥabbᵉḳḗnī

Here the rhyme of lines 1, 2, and 4 is repeated in lines 8 and 9, and into this scheme there is woven the rhyme of lines 6 and 10. A subordinate rhyme or assonance may be found in the repetition of the suffix *-ká* in lines 3, 5, 7.

The following is an attempt to reproduce rhyme and rhythm in English.

'Woúld that thoú wert my bróther,
Who súcked at the breásts of my móther!
When I foúnd thee withoút I would kíss thee,
Nor feár the reproách of anóther;
Would leád thee, would bríng thee
To the hoúse of my móther who traíns me,

Would gíve thee to drínk spiced wíne,
Púre pomegránate, none óther.
—His léft arm is únder my heád,
And seé! his ríght arm enchaíns me.'

The poem of *ch.* 6^{1-3} is complete in itself, and makes use of the masculine plural termination *-ī́m* to furnish a rhyme in lines 2, 7, 8, 10.

'ā́nā hālák dōdḗk
háyyāphā́ bannašī́m
'ā́nā pānā́ dōdḗk
ū́nᵉbaḳšénnu 'immā́k
dōdī́ yārád lᵉgannṓ
lá'ᵃrūgṓt habbṓsem
lir'ṓt bagganní̄m
wᵉlilḳṓṭ šōšanní̄m
'ᵃnī́ lᵉdōdī́ wᵉdṓdī lī́
hārō'ḗ baššṓšanní̄m

Reproducing rhyme and rhythm we may render:

'Whíther has góne thy lóve,
Thoú whom beaúty dówers?
Whíther has túrned thy lóve?
Lét us seék him wíth thee.
My lóve has gone dówn to his gárden,
Dówn to the béds of the spíces,
To shépherd in the bówers
And gáther the flówers.
Í am my lóve's, and my lóve is míne,
Who shépherds amóng the flówers.'

These two poems by no means stand alone as illustrations of the author's partiality for rhyme. Other instances of its employment may be gathered from all parts of the book. Thus in *ch.* 8^{6} we have:

sīmḗnī kaḥōtā́m ʿal libbékā
kaṣṣāmī́d ʿal zᵉrōʿékā
kī ʿazzā́ kammā́wet ʾahᵃbā́
ḳāšā́ kišʾṓl ḳinʾā́
rᵉšāphéhā ríšphē ʾḗš
šalhébetyā́[1]

i.e. (without attempting to reproduce the rhyme):

'Sét me as a seál upon thine heárt,
Ås a brácelet upon thine árm:
For stróng as deáth is lóve,
Hársh as She'ól is jeálousy,
Its bólts are bólts of fíre,
A fláme of Yā́.'

In *ch.* 5[1] every stress-word in each line rhymes with its corresponding word in lines 1 to 4, and there is a similar correspondence between lines 5 and 6:

bā́tī lᵉgannī́ ʾᵃḥōtī́
ʾārī́tī mōrī́ ʿim bᵉsāmī́
ʾākáltī yaʿrī́ ʿim dibšī́
šātī́tī yēnī́ ʿim ḥᵃlābī́
ʾiklū́ rēʿī́m
šikrū́ dōdī́m[2]

'I have éntered my gárden, my síster;
I have gáthered my mýrrh with my bálsam;
I have eáten my cómb with my hóney;
I have drúnk my wíne with my mílk.
Come, eát, O friénds;
Be drúnk with lóve.'

[1] כַּצָּמִיד, 'as a bracelet', is substituted for כַּחוֹתָם, 'as a seal', repeated from the preceding line.

[2] The text adds כַּלָּה, 'bride', after *ʾᵃḥōtī́*, 'my sister' (perhaps a marginal note to explain the reference), and reads in the last line שְׁתוּ וְשִׁכְרוּ, 'drink and be drunk', instead of שִׁכְרוּ merely.

Particularly striking is the use of rhyme in the gnomic sayings of the 'Wise', in which its employment would make an appeal to the popular taste, and form an aid to memory. Numerous examples are to be found throughout the Book of Proverbs, and in the Hebrew text of Ecclesiasticus. Occasionally we find recurrent rhymes in passages of considerable length. Examples of this are:

Prov. 5^{7-14}.

7. *w^{e}ʿattā́ bānī́m šimʿū lī́*
w^{e}ʾal tāsū́rū mḗʾimrē phī́
8. *harḥḗḳ mēʿāléhā darkékā*
w^{e}ʾal tiḳráb ʾel pétaḥ bētā́h
9. *pen tittḗn laʾ^{a}ḥērī́m hōdékā*
ūš^{e}nōtékā l^{e}ʾákzārī́
10. *pen yisb^{e}ʿū́ zārī́m kōḥékā*
waʿ^{a}ṣābéka b^{e}bḗt nokrī́
11. *w^{e}nāhamtā́ b^{e}ʾáḥ^{a}rītékā*
biklṓt b^{e}sār^{e}kā́ ūš^{e}ʾērékā
12. *w^{e}ʾāmartā́*
ʾḗk sānḗtī mūsā́r
w^{e}tōkáḥat nāʾáṣ libbī́
13. *w^{e}lō šāmáʿtī b^{e}ḳṓl mōráy*
w^{e}limlamm^{e}dáy lō hiṭṭī́tī ʾoznī́
14. *kimʿáṭ hāyī́tī b^{e}kol rā́ʿ*
b^{e}tṓk ḳāhā́l w^{e}ʿēdā́

7. 'And nów, O ye sóns, hear mé,
And depárt not from the wórds of my moúth.
8. Remóve far fróm her thy wáy,
And approách not the doór of her hoúse;
9. Lest thou gíve to óthers thine hónour,
And thy yeárs to óne without rúth;

10. Lest stráńgers be fílled with thy stréngth,
And thy lábours be in the hoúse of an álien;

11. And thou gróan in thy látter énd,
When thy bódy and thy flésh are consúmed,

12. And sáy,
"Hów have I háted instrúction,
And my heárt despísed reproóf,

13. Neither have I obéyed the voíce of my teáchers,
Nor to my instrúctors have I inclíned mine eár!

14. Well nígh have I cóme to all íll
In the mídst of the congregátion and assémbly".'

Here the combination of rhyme with the three-beat rhythm makes the passage go with a fine swing. The interlacing of the rhymes is most skilful and effective. Very striking in the distichs of *vv.* 9,10,13 is the way in which the rhyme of the last-stressed word of the first line is taken up and reinforced by the first-stressed word of the parallel line (*hōdékā—ūšᵉnōtékā*; *kōḥékā—waʿᵃṣābékā*[1]; *mōráy—wᵉlimlammᵉdāy*). In the last instance:

wᵉlō šāmáʿtī bᵉḳṓl mōráy
wᵉlimlammᵉdáy lō hiṭṭī́tī 'oznī́,

[1] We may notice that, in these two examples, we have proof (if that be thought to be necessary) that the pausal system of the Massoretes is not a late invention, but is primitive. All the rhymed endings in ֶךָ, *-ékā*, 'thy', at the end of lines are attached to *singulars*, and, if they did not stand in pause, would take the form ְךָ, *-ᵉkā́*; e.g. *hōdᵉkā́*, 'thine honour'. In order to form a reinforcing rhyme in the first stress-syllable of the parallel stichos which is *not* in pause, the poet has to use *plural* forms (*šᵉnōtékā*, 'thy years', *ʿᵃṣābékā*, 'thy labours') in which the suffix is ֶיךָ, *-ékā*, whether the word is non-pausal or pausal.

which we may in a measure reproduce by rendering,

'Neither have I obéyed the voíce of my teáchers,
Nor to my preáchers have I inclíned my eár,'

wᵉlimlammᵉdáy follows upon *mōráy* almost like a great clash of bells, and is intended, we may conjecture, to reproduce the loud iteration of the warnings addressed to the sinner—all to no effect.

Ecclus. 13^{4-7}.

'ím tiḳšar lṓ yáʿᵃbōd bā́k
wᵉ'im tikráʿ yaḥmṓl ʿālékā
'im yeš lᵉkā́ yēṭíb dᵉbārā́w ʿimmā́k
wīrōšeškā́ wᵉlṓ yik'ab lṓ
ṣōrek lṓ ʿimmᵉkā́ wᵉhḗšaʿ lā́k
wᵉsiḥḥḗḳ lᵉkā́ wᵉhibtīḥékā
ʿad 'ᵃšér yōʿíl yᵉhā́tēl bā́k
paʿᵃmáyim šālṓš yaʿᵃrīṣékā
ūbᵉkḗn yir'ᵃkā́ wᵉhitʿábbēr bā́k
ūbᵉrōšṓ yānī́ᵃʿ 'ēlḗkā[1]

'If thou sérvest his túrn, he will máke thee his sláve,
But if thou faílest, he will lét thee alóne;
If thou hást, he will gíve thee the faírest of wórds,
And will fleéce thee withoút remórse.
Hath he neéd of theé? He will flátter thee wéll,
And will jóke thee, and caúse thee to trúst him;
As lóng as it sérve, he will máke thee his spórt,
Twíce, yea thríce, will he cheát thee;
And thén he will seé thee and páss thee bý,
And will sháke his heád at thy plíght.'

Cf. also the rhymes in *vv.*[16abcd,17b,18a,23ab] of the passage from Ecclus. 38 quoted on p. 52.

[1] The position of the stress-accents in this passage, particularly in the first four lines, is peculiarly difficult to decide.

Very commonly the verses fall into quatrains, which may contain rhymes in two, three, or (more rarely) in all four of the lines. Examples are:

Prov. $1^{15,16}$.

b^{e}nī́ 'al tēlḗk b^{e}dérek 'ittā́m
m^{e}nā́ʿ ragl^{e}kā́ minn^{e}tībōtā́m
kī raglēhém lārā́ʿ yārū́ṣū
wī́mah^{a}rū́ lišpok dā́m

'My són, do not gó in the wáy with thém;
Withhóld thy foót from their dévious páths:
For their feét do rún unto évil,
Ánd they make speéd to shed bloód.'

Ecclus. 6^{25-27}.

háṭ šikm^{e}kā́ w^{e}sā́'éhā
w^e'al taḳōṣ b^{e}taḥbū́lōtéhā
d^{e}rōš waḥ^{a}ḳōr baḳḳēš ūm^{e}ṣā́
w^{e}héḥ^{e}zaḳtā́h w^e'al tarpéhā

'Bów down thy shoúlder and beár her,
And bé not thou cháfed by her coúnsels;
Reseárch and explóre, seek oút and attaín,
And grásp her and dó not reléase her.'

The following forms of rhymed quatrains are to be found in these books:

Rhyming 1, 2, 3, 4. Ecclus. 4^{29-30}, 12^{12}, 35^{24-25}, 36^{18-19}.
Rhyming 1, 2, 3; non-rhyming 4. Prov. 2^{6-7}, 5^{3-4}, 22^{18-19}; Ecclus. 9^{6-7}, 13^{15-16}, 16^{11-12}, 36^{20-21}.
Rhyming 1, 2, 4; non-rhyming 3. Prov. 1^{15-16}, 3^{13-14}; Ecclus. 4^{22-23}, 6^{25-27}, 46^{19}.
Rhyming 1, 3, 4; non-rhyming 2. Prov. 3^{7-8}, 3^{21-22}; Ecclus. 9^{1-2}, 9^{15-16}, 14^{23-24}, 16^{24-25}, 31^{4}.
Rhyming 2, 3, 4; non-rhyming 1. Prov. 4^{20-21}, 7^{2-3} Ecclus. 14^{1-2}.

Rhyming 1, 2, and 3, 4. Ecclus. 30^{23}, 38^{16}.

Rhyming 1, 3, and 2, 4. Prov. 5^{9-10}, 13^{24-25} (if a quatrain, and not two unconnected distichs).

Rhyming 1, 4, and 2, 3. Prov. 2^{2-3}.

Rhyming 1, 4; non-rhyming 2, 3. Prov. 3^{5-6}, 3^{23-24}, 4^{8-9}, 4^{12-13}, 5^{17-18}, 7^{8-9}; Ecclus. 46^{9}.

Rhyming 2, 3; non-rhyming 1, 4. Prov. 23^{1-2}; Ecclus. 11^{8-9}.

Rhyming 2, 4; non-rhyming 1, 3. Prov. 4^{24-25}, 5^{12-13}; Ecclus. 9^{3}, 15^{2-3}, 15^{7-8}, $16^{7-8,9-10}$, 41^{9}, 43^{28-29}, 45^{19}.

Examination of the rhymes offered by these specimens of gnomic poetry reveals a development in method. In the specimens of folk-poetry first cited the rhyme is produced by the use of identical suffix-forms, *-ī́* 'my', *-ékā* 'thy', &c., or the fem. sing. termination *-ā́*, or the plural terminations masc. *-ī́m*, fem. *-ṓt*, in combination with the varying radical preceding. The only exception is the rhyme on the termination *-ṓn* in the names Heshbón, Sihón, Arnón in Num. 21^{28}. In Proverbs and Ecclesiasticus, however, while the great majority of rhymes are produced by this method, we further find abundant evidence of an attempt to produce rhyme by the use of words with *unrelated terminations*. The following are examples:

1. The suffix ־ִי *-ī́* 'my' rhymed with a formative termination *-ī́*. Prov. 5^{7-14} לִי *lī́* 'to me', פִּי *pī́*, 'my mouth', &c., rhymed with אַכְזָרִי *'akzārī́* 'cruel', נָכְרִי *nokrī́* 'alien'.

2. The suffix ־ָהּ *-ā́h*, 'her' rhymed with the fem. sing. termination ־ָה *-ā́*. Prov. 3^{13-14} תְּבוּאָתָהּ *tᵉbū'ātā́h* 'her produce' rhymed with חָכְמָה *ḥokmā́* 'wisdom', תְּבוּנָה *tᵉbūnā́* 'understanding'; Prov. 5^{3-4} חִכָּהּ *ḥikkā́h* 'her palate' with זָרָה *zārā́* 'a strange woman', לַעֲנָה *la'ᵃnā́*

'wormwood'; Prov. 7^{8-9} פִּנָּהּ *pinnáh* 'her corner' with אֲפֵלָה *'ᵃphēlá* 'darkness'; Prov. 9^{1} בֵּיתָהּ *bētáh* 'her house' with שִׁבְעָה *šib'á* 'seven'; Prov. 31^{26} לְשׁוֹנָהּ *lᵉšōnáh* 'her tongue' with חָכְמָה *ḥokmá* 'wisdom'.

3. The suffix ־ָהּ *-áh* 'her' rhymed with a radical ל״א verbal form. Prov. 8^{1} קוֹלָהּ *ḳōláh* 'her voice' with תִּקְרָא *tiḳrá* 'she calls'; Prov. 31^{10} מִכְרָהּ *mikráh* 'her price' with תִּמְצָא *timṣá* 'can find'.

4. The suffix ־ֶיהָ *-éhā* 'her' apparently rhymed with a ל guttural 3rd fem. perfect pausal form in Prov. 2^{17} נְעוּרֶיהָ *nᵉ'ūréhā* 'her youth', שָׁכֵחָה *šākéḥā* 'she has forgotten'.

5. The suffix ־ָם *-ám* 'their' rhymed with a radical form. In Prov. $1^{15,16}$ with דָּם *dám* 'blood'; in Ecclus. 44^{1-8} with עוֹלָם *'ōlám* 'eternity'.

6. The fem. sing. termination ־ָה *-á* rhymed with a radical form. Prov. $2^{2b,3a}$ תְּבוּנָה *tᵉbūná* 'understanding' with תִּקְרָא *tiḳrá* 'thou callest'; Prov. 9^{13} הֹמִיָּה *hōmiyyá* 'noisy' with מָה *má* 'anything'.

7. A formative termination rhymed with a radical form. Prov. 1^{11} חִנָּם *ḥinnám* 'causeless' (*-ám* formative) with דָּם *dám* 'blood'; Ecclus. 36^{29} קִנְיָן *ḳinyán* 'possession' (*-án* formative) with מִשְׁעָן *miš'án* 'support' (from root *ša'án* with preformative מ).

8. Two radical forms with accidentally rhyming terminations. Prov. 13^{24-25} מוּסָר *mūsár* 'instruction', תֶּחְסָר *teḥsár* 'shall lack'; Prov. 21^{12} רָשָׁע *rāšá'* 'wicked', רָע *rá'* 'evil'; Ecclus. 6^{3} תְּשָׁרֵשׁ *tᵉšārḗš* 'it will uproot', יָבֵשׁ *yābḗš* 'withered'; Ecclus. 7^{18} בִּמְחִיר *bimḥír* 'for a price', אוֹפִיר *'Ophír* (place-name); Ecclus. 7^{21} כְּנָפֶשׁ *kᵉnápheš* 'like (your)self', חָפֶשׁ *ḥápheš* 'freedom'; Ecclus. 11^{7} תְּסַלֵּף *tᵉsalléph* 'subvert', תְּזַיֵּף *tazzéph* 'rebuke'; Ecclus. $11^{8b,9a}$ תְּדַבֵּר *tᵉdabbér* 'speak', תְּאַחֵר *tᵉ'aḥḥér* 'tarry' (*si vera lectio*).

Turning now to Aramaic, we may observe that, while possessing the same facilities as Hebrew for forming rhyme out of identical terminations, such as pronominal suffixes, the feminine singular termination, and the terminations of the masculine and feminine plural, it possesses a further peculiarity which renders the production of rhyme even easier to it than to the other language. This is seen in the fact that the place of the prepositive Definite Article in Hebrew is taken in Aramaic by the postpositive *Emphatic State*. While in Hebrew two substantives of dissimilar endings, such as *mélek* 'king', *'ébed* 'slave', become with the Definite Article *ham-mélek* 'the king', *hā-'ébed* 'the slave', and so remain unrhymable; in Aramaic the cognate substantives *mᵉlḗk*, *'ᵃbḗd* become in the Emphatic State *malkā́* 'the king', *'abdā́* 'the slave', and thus are susceptible of rhyme. Moreover, since in the plural the indefinite *malkī́n*, *'abdī́n* become in the Emphatic State *malkayyā́*, *'abdayyā́*, it is obvious that rhyme may be formed between a singular and a plural form if both are in the Emphatic State. For instance, *malkā́* can be rhymed with *'abdayyā́*. This increased facility for rhyming may certainly be held to have rendered rhyme the more ready of adoption, especially in sayings of a gnomic character formed upon the Hebrew model.

It has been remarked verbally to the present writer with reference to the examples presently to be cited, that our Lord could not have spoken as He did without forming rhyme, i.e. that the rhymes may be considered an accidental phenomenon. It is true that the existence of rhyme is closely bound up with the parallelistic form of the sayings; yet to view the rhymes as purely accidental, i.e. to hold that the Speaker was unconscious or negligent of the fact that He was making them, is surely a very unlikely hypothesis. The great bulk of the Hebrew poetry of the Old Testament, while parallelistic in form, is unmarked by the use of rhyme. It is only, as we have seen, in certain forms of Hebrew poetry—popular folk-poetry and gnomic teaching—that rhyme is markedly characteristic; and here its employment is evidently due to design. It may be held, then, that when rhyme occurs in our Lord's parallelistic teaching, it is equally due to design, and was adopted as likely to aid the memory of His hearers.

The first example of our Lord's use of rhyme which we may notice is found in the Lord's Prayer, an Aramaic rendering of which has already been given on p. 113.

'^{a}būnán d^{e}bišmayyā́ Our Father Who (art) in heaven	*yitḳaddáš š^{e}mā́k* let be hallowed Thy name
tētḗ malkūtā́k let come Thy Kingdom	*t^{e}hḗ ṣibyōnā́k* let be Thy will
hēkmā́ d^{e}bišmayyā́ as in heaven	*hēkdḗn b^{e}'ar'ā́* so on earth
laḥmán d^{e}yōmā́ Our bread of the day	*hab lán yōmā dḗn* give to us day this
ūš^{e}bōḳ lán ḥōbḗn and forgive to us our debts	*hēk dišbáḳnan l^{e}ḥayyābḗn* as we have forgiven our debtors
w^{e}lā ta'lī́nan l^{e}nisyōnā́ and not lead us into temptation	*'ellā paṣṣī́nan min bīšā́*[1] but deliver us from evil.

[1] The apocopated pronominal suffix of the 1st pers. pl. *-ḗn*, which we have adopted in *ḥōbḗn* 'our debts', *ḥayyābḗn* 'our debtors' (like normal Syriac *ḥawbain, ḥayyābain*), is used in Galilaean Aramaic, as well as the fuller form *-ēnan*; cf. Dalman, *Gramm.*^{2}, §§ 14, 18 (p. 95). Its use here rather than that of the uncontracted form is rendered probable by the fact that it offers an accurate rhyme to *dḗn* in stichos 1 *b*. The Perfect *š^{e}báḳnan*, 'we have forgiven', might also

Here we observe a remarkably elaborate system of rhyme. In the first stichos of tristich 1 the rhyming endings are set, as it were, in *-ā́* st. 1 *a*, *-ā́k* st. 1 *b*. St. 1 *a* is then rhymed in st. 3 *a*, 3 *b*, and st. 1 *b* in st. 2 *a*, 2 *b*. Precisely the same method is followed in tristich 2, where the rhyming ending *-ā́* in st. 1 *a* is followed in st. 3 *a*, 3 *b*, and *-ḗn* in st. 1 *b* is followed in st. 2 *a*, 2 *b*. Moreover, there are instances in some of the stichoi of rhyme of the 3rd stress-syllable with the 1st. Thus in tristich 1, st. 2 *tᵉhḗ* rhymes with *tēṭḗ*, and in tristich 2, st. 1 *hab lán* with *laḥmán*, st. 3 *paṣṣī́nan* with *taʿlī́nan*. And the opening half-stichos of tristich 2 *laḥmán dᵉyōmā́* rhymes stress for stress with the corresponding opening of tristich 1 *'ᵃbūnán dᵉbišmayyā́*.

That rhyme was employed in Jewish prayers in or about our Lord's time can be shown. The *Tᵉphillā* ('prayer') *par excellence* is the *Shᵉmōneh-ʿesrēh*, i.e. 'Eighteen', so called from its eighteen supplications, each rounded off with an appropriate benediction. This prayer, which is written in Hebrew, is in part considerably older than our Lord's time, since discussion arose as to the use of certain of its sections between the schools of Hillel and Shammai. Some of its sections contain indications which point to the period after the destruction of Jerusalem by Titus in A.D. 70; but the whole was completed and bore the name *Shᵉmōneh-ʿesrēh* in the days of Gamaliel II, *c.* A.D. 100. There are two recensions, a Palestinian and a Babylonian, with considerable variations, the

have been contracted *šᵉbáḳn* (as in Syriac); but on the supposition that the uncontracted form שבקנן was used, we have an explanation of the variants Matt. ἀφήκαμεν = שְׁבַקְנַן, *šᵉbaḳnan* (Perfect), Luke ἀφίομεν = שָׁבְקִינַן *šābᵉḳīnan* (Participle with pronoun), the difference being one of vocalization merely.

latter increased to nineteen sections, by addition of a prayer against apostates.[1]

The following examples of rhyme are taken from the Palestinian recension. Section 2 forms rhyme upon the masc. plural termination *-ím*.

'attá gibbṓr mašpíl gē'ím
ḥāzā́ḳ ūmēdī́n 'ārīṣím
ḥḗ 'ōlāmím mēḳím mētím
maššíb hārū́ᵃḥ ūmōríd haṭṭál
mᵉkalkḗl ḥayyím mᵉḥayyé hammētím
kᵉhéreph 'áyin yᵉšū'á lā́nū taṣmíaḥ
bārū́k 'attá 'ᵃdōnáy mᵉḥayyé hammētím[2]

'Míghty art Thoú, abásing the proúd,
Stróng, and júdging the rúthless,
Líving for áye, raísing the deád,
Sénding the wínd, and drópping the déw,
Noúrishing the líving, quíckening the deád.
As in the twínkling of an éye Thou wilt caúse for
us salvátion to spring fórth.
Bléssed art Thoú, O Lórd that quíckenest the deád.'

[1] Cf. for the above-given statements the full references cited by Strack and Billerbeck, *Das Evangelium nach Matthäus erläutert aus Talmud und Midrasch* (1922), pp. 406 ff. A short account of the prayer, with a translation, is given by Schürer, *History of the Jewish People*, Div. II, vol. ii, pp. 83 ff. The Hebrew text may conveniently be consulted in O. Holtzmann's edition of *Berakot*, pp. 10 ff.

[2] The second and third lines convey the impression that they ought to be stressed:

ḥāzā́ḳ ūmḗdīn 'ā́rīṣím
ḥē 'ṓlāmím mḗḳīm mētím,

the strong countertone on the initial syllable of *'ā́rīṣím* throwing back the accent of *ūmēdī́n*, and in *'ṓlāmím* annulling the accent of the preceding *ḥḗ*.

In section 3 we have rhyme on the masc. singular suffix *-ékā*.

ḳādṓš 'attā́ wᵉnōrā́ šᵉmékā
wᵉ'ēn 'ᵉlṓᵃh mibbál'ādékā
bārū́k 'attā́ 'ᵃdōnā́y hā'ḗl haḳḳādṓš

'Hóly art Thoú, and feárful Thy náme,
And there is nót a Gód apárt from Theé.
Bléssed art Thoú, O Lórd, the hóly Gód.'

Section 8 offers rhyme upon the 1st pers. plur. suffix *-ḗnū*.

rᵉphā'ḗnū 'ᵃdōnā́y 'ᵉlōhḗnū mimmak'ṓb libbḗnu
wᵉyāgṓn wa'ᵃnāḥā́ ha'ᵃbḗr mimménnu
wᵉha'ᵃlḗ rᵉphū'ā́ lᵉmákkōtḗnū
bārū́k 'attā́ rōphḗ ḥōlḗ 'ammṓ yisrā'ḗl

'Heál us, O Lórd our Gód, of the afflíction of our heárt,
And griéf and síghing remóve from ús,
And admínister heáling únto our woúnds.
Bléssed art Thoú that heálest the síck of Thy peóple Ísrael.'

The Babylonian recension likewise offers marked examples of the use of rhyme.

In section 5 this is formed on the masc. singular suffix *-ékā*.

hᵃšībḗnū 'ābī́nū lᵉtṓrātékā
wᵉḳārᵉbḗnū malkḗnū la'ᵃbṓdātékā
wᵉhaḥᵃzīrḗnū bitšūbā́ šᵉlēmā́ lᵉphānékā
bārū́k 'attā́ 'ᵃdōnā́y hārōṣé bitšūbā́

'Bring us báck, O our Fáther, únto Thy láw;
And bring us neár, O our Kíng, únto Thy sérvice;
And make us retúrn in fúll repéntance before Theé.
Bléssed art Thoú, O Lórd, Who art pleásed with repéntance.'

Section 6 rhymes upon the 1st plur. Perfect verbal form.

s^e^laḥ lā́nū 'ābī́nū kī ḥāṭā́nū
m^e^ḥōl lā́nū malkḗnū kī phāšā́'nū
kī 'ēl ṭṓb w^e^sallā́ḥ 'ā́ttā
bārū́k 'attā́ '^a^dōnā́y ḥannū́n hammarbé lislṓ^a^ḥ

'Forgíve us, O our Fáther, for we have sínned;
Párdon us, O our Kíng, for we have transgréssed;
For a goód God and forgíving art Thoú.
Bléssed art Thoú, O Lórd the mérciful, Who forgívest abúndantly.'

In both these examples we observe a tendency to obtain rhyme or assonance, not merely between the closing stress-syllables of parallel stichoi, but between corresponding stress-syllables within the stichoi. We have noticed the same phenomenon in the Lord's Prayer.

In section 10 we have rhyme upon the suffix of the 1st plur.

t^e^ḳā́' b^e^šōphā́r gādṓl l^e^ḥērūtḗnū
w^e^sā nḗs l^e^ḳabbḗṣ 'et kṓl gāliyyōtḗnū
mē'arbā́' kanphṓt hā'ā́reṣ l^e^'arṣḗnū
bārū́k 'attā́ '^a^dōnā́y m^e^ḳabbḗṣ nidḥḗ 'ammṓ yisrā'ḗl

'Blów with great trúmpet for oúr releáse,
And raise bánner to gáther the whóle of our éxiled,
From the foúr extrémities of the eárth unto our lánd.
Bléssed art Thoú, O Lórd, Who gátherest the oútcasts of the peóple Ísrael.'

A secondary interior rhyme, which, if accidental, is at any rate striking and effective, is that between *gādṓl* and *'et kṓl.*

The Beatitudes, according to Matthew's version (Matt. 5^{3-11}), exhibit clear indications of composition in rhyme, and (in the main) three-stress rhythm. The final one, however, which is differently constructed (2nd person for 3rd, and no specific promise attached) is neither rhyming nor rhythmical. The first eight may be rendered as follows.

1. *ṭūbēhōn mískᵉnayyā́ [bᵉrūḥā́]*
Their happiness the poor [in spirit],
dᵉdīlᵉhōn malkūtā́ dišmayyā́
for theirs (is) the kingdom of heaven.

2. *ṭūbēhōn dᵉmít'abbᵉlī́n*
Their happiness that (are) mourning,
dᵉhinnū́n mítnaḥḥᵃmī́n
for they (shall be) comforted.

3. *ṭūbēhōn 'inwā́nayyā́*
Their happiness the meek,
dᵉhinnū́n yērᵉtū́n lᵉar'ā́
for they shall inherit the earth.

4. *ṭūbēhōn dᵉkāphᵉnī́n wᵉṣāḥáyin [lᵉṣidḳā́]*
Their happiness that (are) hungering and thirsting [for righteousness],
dᵉhinnū́n mitmᵉláyin
for they (shall be) filled.

5. *ṭūbēhōn raḥmā́nayyā́*
Their happiness the merciful,
da'ᵃlēhōn hāwáyin raḥmayyā́
for upon them being the mercies.

6. *ṭūbēhōn didkáyin bᵉlibbā́*
Their happiness that (are) pure in heart,
dᵉhinnū́n ḥāmáyin lēlāhā́
for they (shall be) seeing God.

7. *ṭūbēhōn dᵉ'ābᵉdī́n šᵉlāmā́*
Their happiness that (are) making peace,
dᵉyitḳᵉrṓn bᵉnṓy dēlāhā́
for they shall be called His sons of God.

8. *ṭūbēhōn dirdīphī́n bᵉgḗn dᵉṣidḳā́*
Their happiness that (are) persecuted because of righteousness,
dᵉdīlᵉhōn malkūtā́ dišmayyā́
for theirs (is) the kingdom of heaven.

Here we note that in no. 1 rhythm favours omission of *τῷ πνεύματι*, as in Luke 6^{20}. The addition is almost certainly an editorial gloss to explain that 'the poor' are not merely those who are deficient in material goods; but since the allusion is to the *ʿaniyyīm* of the Old Testament (a Hebrew term which is variously rendered by A.V. 'poor', 'afflicted', 'humble', 'lowly'), the full connotation of the term would be clear to our Lord's audience apart from such explanation. The specific reference is to Isa. 61^{1} (cf. Luke 4^{18} *εὐαγγελίσασθαι πτωχοῖς*), where the Massoretic Text has 'the meek' עֲנָוִים *ʿanāwīm*, a term which frequently throughout the Old Testament interchanges with עֲנִיִּים *ʿaniyyīm* (which is the reading of the LXX and Arabic versions in this passage). The two terms are closely related in meaning; *ʿanāwīm* (Aram. *ʿinwānayyā* = *οἱ πραεῖς* in Beatitude no. 3) being a stative form, better rendered 'humble' (towards God) rather than 'meek';[1] while *ʿaniyyīm* is the corresponding passive form, and properly means 'humbled' by external circumstances, such as the persecution of the ungodly. The *ʿaniyyīm* are 'humbled' because they are *ʿanāwīm* 'humble' towards God—i.e. because for religious motives (their attitude towards God) they refuse to take steps to avenge themselves or assert their personal rights.

In no. 4 both rhythm and rhyme speak conclusively for the original omission of *τὴν δικαιοσύνην*, an explanation which is hardly more necessary here than it would

[1] Moses is the typical Old Testament instance of a man who was *ʿānāw* (Num. 12^{3}; cf. Ecclus. 45^{4}); yet he certainly was not what we understand by the term 'meek' (the reading of A.V., R.V.). The proper meaning of the term is seen, in the case in point, in his refusal to take steps to vindicate himself against Aaron and Miriam, and in his leaving his vindication to God.

be in Isa. 55 [1ff.] ('Ho, every one that thirsteth', &c.), a passage which was probably in our Lord's mind when He framed the beatitude. In the promise attached to this beatitude we notice the only occurrence of a two-stress in place of a three-stress stichos; and, while it is by no means necessary to postulate absolute rhythmical uniformity, we may conjecture that possibly some such term as *ṭāb* 'good' may have been accidentally omitted—*dᵉhinnūn ṭáb mitmᵉláyin* 'For they shall be filled with good' would connect still more closely with Isa. 55[2], 'hearken diligently unto Me, and eat ye that which is good', than the passage does at present.

In no. 5 *raḥmayya* '*the* mercies' are specifically the mercies of God, which is clearly the sense intended by ἐλεηθήσονται. The rendering here adopted is precisely that of Pal. Syr.

It is only when we reach no. 8 that we are faced by a somewhat unwieldy line of four stresses; and the possibility suggests itself that this may originally have run *ṭūbēhṓn dᵉrādᵉphīn lᵉṣidḳā́*, 'Blessed are they that pursue righteousness', the Old Testament connexion in thought being with Deut. 16[20], 'Righteousness, righteousness shalt thou pursue, that thou mayest live, and inherit the land which Yahweh thy God giveth thee' (cf. also Isa. 51[1], 'ye that pursue righteousness'). The prep. *lᵉ* in *lᵉṣidḳā*, which introduces the direct accusative, may then have been misunderstood in the sense '*for*', and this may have led to the understanding of רדפין as passive רְדִיפִין *rᵉdīphīn* 'persecuted' (lit. 'pursued') instead of active רָדְפִין *rādᵉphīn* 'pursuing'.

There are frequent instances of rhyme in the teaching of our Lord, especially when it is couched in proverbial form.

Matt. 7^{6}.

lā tīh^{a}búṇ ḳudšā́ l^{e}kalbayyā́
Do not give the holy thing to the dogs

w^{e}lā tirmū́n margālyātkṓn ḳ^{o}dām ḥ^{a}zīrayyā́
and do not cast your pearls before the swine

d^{e}lā y^{e}dū́šūn 'innṓn b^{e}raglēhṓn
lest they trample them with their feet

wītū́būn wībázz$^{e'}$ūnkṓn
and turn and rend you

Luke 6$^{27-29}$. Cf. Matt. 5^{39,40}.

raḥ^{a}mū́n l^{e}ba'^{a}lē d^{e}bābēkṓn — *ṭayy^{e}bū́n l^{e}sān$^{e'}$ēkṓn*
Love your enemies — do good to your haters

bār^{e}kū́n l^{e}lāṭēkṓn — *ṣallṓn 'al rād^{e}phēkṓn*
bless your cursers — pray for your persecutors

lidmāḥ^{e}yā́k 'al liss^{e}tā́ — *ḳār^{e}bū́n 'ūph ḥūr^{e}nā́*
to thy smiter on the cheek — present also the other

ūmin man d^{e}šāḳḗl marṭūṭā́k lā tiklḗ 'ūph kittūnā́k[1]
and from one that takes thy cloak do not withhold also thy coat.

Matt. 8^{20} = Luke 9^{58}.

l^{e}ta'layyā́ 'īt l^{e}hṓn bōrī́n
To the foxes are to them holes

le'ōphā́ dišmayyā́ ḳinnī́n
to the birds of the heavens nests

ūl^{e}bár '^{e}nāšā́ lēt lḗh
but to the Son of man is not to Him

hā́n d^{e}yarkḗn rēšḗh
where He may lay His head

[1] In this passage it would be possible, for the most part, to regard each line as properly consisting of two-parallel three-beat stichoi, e.g.

raḥ^{a}mū́n l^{e}ba'^{a}lḗ debābēkṓn
ṭayy^{e}bū́n l^{e}sā́n$^{e'}$ēkṓn.

The consideration which guides us to regard it rather as a single four-beat stichos, parallel with the similar stichos which accompanies it, is Rabbi Azariah's theory of *Things and their Parts* as a guide to rhythmical structure (cf. p. 59). Each half-line regularly consists of two parts of a proposition, e.g. verb and object; and thus regarded offers two stresses and not more.

With this ready rhyming response to a remark made by some one else we may compare a passage in the Fourth Gospel.

John $6^{26,27}$.

bāʿēttū́n lī lā d^{e}ʿātī́n ḥ^{a}mētū́n
Ye are seeking Me not because signs ye saw

'ellā da'^{a}kaltū́n min laḥmā́ ūs^{e}baʿtū́n
but because ye ate of the bread and were sated

lā taʿm^{e}lū́n l^{e}mēkūltā́ d^{e}ʿāb^{e}rā́
do not toil for the food which perishes

'ellā l^{e}mēkūltā́ dilʿālám[1] *m^{e}katt^{e}rā́*
but for the food which for ever abides

d^{e}yīhā́b l^{e}kṓn bar '^{e}nāšā́
which shall give to you the Son of man

hū d^{e}ḥatmḗh 'abbā́ '^{e}lāhā́
Him whom has sealed Him the Father God

Matt. 15^{14} = Luke 6^{39}.

'īn yidbár samyā́ l^{e}samyā
If shall lead the blind the blind

t^{e}rēhṓn nāph^{e}lī́n b^{e}gumṣā́
both of them (shall be) falling into the ditch

Luke 9^{62}.

man d^{e}rāmḗ y^{e}dḗh ʿal paddānā́
Whoso puts his hand on the plough

umístakkál la'^{a}ḥōrā́
and gazes backwards

lēt šāwḗ l^{e}malkūtḗh dēlāhā́
is not meet for His Kingdom of God

Luke $12^{33,34}$.

ḳinyānēkṓn zabb^{e}nū́n Your goods sell	*w^{e}ṣidḳā́ h^{a}bū́n* and alms give
ʿubdū́n l^{e}kōn kīsā́n make to you scrips	*d^{e}lā́ bāl^{e}yā́n* that not (are) wearing out

[1] Greek εἰς ζωὴν αἰώνιον. Cf. foot-note, p. 106.

sīmā́ bišmayyā́ — *d^{e}lā́ sāy^{e}phā́*
a treasure in the heavens — that not (is) failing

hān d^{e}gannābī́n lā ḳār^{e}bī́n — *w^{e}sāsī́n lā sār^{e}ḥī́n*
where thieves not (are) approaching — and moths not (are) corrupting

d^{e}hā́n sīmatkṓn — *'ūph tammā́n libb^{e}kṓn*
for where your treasure — also there your heart

Here we observe rhyme, not merely between stress-syllables 2 and 4 of corresponding half-stichoi, but, in stichoi 3–5, between stress-syllables 1 and 3 (*sīmā́—d^{e}lā́*; *gannābī́n—sīsī́n*; *hā́n—tammā́n*).

Notice also the recurrence of the rhyme made by the termination *-ā́* of the emphatic state in the translations of Matt. 5^{14-16}, $6^{22,23}$ given on pp. 130, 131. This may be accidental merely; yet it has all the emphasis of design as we read the passages.

The great passage from Q, Matt. 11^{25-27} = Luke $10^{21,22}$, forms a rhythmical poem which rhymes regularly couplet by couplet, if we may assume that the words supplied in angular brackets, parallel to and resumptive of 'I give thanks to Thee' in stichos 1, may have fallen out in transmission. The omission of καὶ συνετῶν, as a doublet of σοφῶν, is suggested on rhythmical grounds.

mōdḗnā lā́k 'abbā́
I give thanks to Thee, O Father,

mārḗ dišmayyā́ ūd^e'ar'ā́
Lord of heaven and of earth,

diṭmárt hāllḗn min ḥakkīmī́n [w^{e}sokl^{e}tānī́n]
that[1] hast hidden these things from wise men [and prudent],

w^{e}gallī́t 'innū́n l^{e}ṭalyī́n
and hast revealed them to children.

'īn 'abbā́ ⟨m^{e}šabbáḥnā lā́k⟩
Yea, Father, ⟨I give glory to Thee⟩

[1] Here 'that' may have the force of 'because', as in the Greek, or it may represent the relative 'who'.

dikdēn ra'ᵃwā́ ḳᵉdāmā́k
because thus it was pleasing before Thee.

kullā́ mᵉsīr lī́ min 'abbā́
Everything (is) delivered to Me from the Father,

wᵉlēt makkḗr librā́ 'ellā 'abbā́,
and there is not (any) knowing the Son but the Father,

wᵉlēt makkḗr lᵉ'abbā́ 'ellā bᵉrā́
and there is not (any) knowing the Father but the Son,

ūman dᵉṣābḗ lēh bᵉrā́ limgallāyā́
and whoso that willeth to him the Son to reveal.

In the parable of the Sheep and the Goats (Matt. 25[31 ff.]) the rhyme or assonance of the similar endings is very marked. The following is a translation of the first half of the parable.

kad yētḗ bar 'ᵉnāšā́ bīḳārḗh
When shall come the Son of Man in His glory

wᵉkū́l mal'ākayyā́ 'immḗh
and all the angels with Him

bᵉkēn yittḗb 'al kursᵉyā́ dīḳārḗh
then shall He sit on the throne of His glory

wᵉyitkannᵉšū́n ḳᵉdāmṓy kul 'amᵉmayyā́
and shall be gathered before Him all the nations

wᵉyaphrēšinnṓn gᵉbā́r min ḥabrḗh
and He shall separate them a man from his fellow

kᵉmā dᵉmaphrḗš ra'ᵃyā́ lᵉ'immᵉrayyā́
as (is) separating the shepherd the sheep

min bēnḗ gᵉdayyā́
from among the goats

wīḳī́m lᵉ'immᵉrayyā́ min yammīnḗh
and shall set the sheep on His right hand

wᵉligdayyā́ min sᵉmālḗh
and the goats on His left hand

bᵉkēn yēmar malkā lᵉhinnūn dᵉmin yammīnēh
Then shall say the King to those who (are) on His right hand

'ētṓ bᵉrīkṓy dᵉ'abbā
Come His blessed of the Father

'aḥsī́nū malkūtā́ da'^{a}tīdā́ l^{e}kṓn
inherit the kingdom which (was) prepared for you

min y^{e}sōdḗh d^{e}'āl^{e}mā́
from its foundation of the world

b^{e}gḗn dikphanī́t w^{e}'ōkaltū́nī
because I was hungry and ye fed Me

ṣ^{e}ḥḗt w^{e}'aškḳītū́nī
I was thirsty and ye watered Me

'aksā́n h^{a}wḗt ūk^{e}naštū́nī
a stranger was I and ye housed Me

'arṭīláy w^{e}'albeštū́nī
naked and ye clothed Me

m^{e}raʿ h^{a}wēt w^{e}'asʿertū́nī
sick was I and ye visited Me

baḥ^{a}būšyā́ w^{e}'alwītū́nī
in prison and ye joined Me.

b^{e}kēn m^{e}gībīn lēh ṣaddīḳayyā w^{e}'ām^{e}rīn
Then (shall be) answering Him the righteous and saying

māran
Lord

'ēmātáy ḥ^{a}mēnātā́k kāphḗn w^{e}'ōkalnātā́k
When saw we Thee hungry and fed Thee

w^{e}ṣāḥḗ w^{e}'aškḳīnātā́k
and thirsty and watered Thee

'ēmātáy ḥ^{a}mēnātā́k 'aksā́n ūk^{e}našnātā́k
when saw we Thee a stranger and housed Thee

w^{e}'arṭīláy w^{e}'albēšnātā́k
and naked and clothed Thee

'ēmātáy ḥ^{a}mēnātā́k m^{e}rā́ʿ ⟨w^{e}'as'ernātā́k⟩
when saw we Thee sick ⟨and visited Thee⟩

ūbaḥ^{a}būšyā́ w^{e}'alwīnātā́k
and in prison and joined Thee

ūm^{e}gīb malkā w^{e}'āmar l^{e}hōn
and (shall be) answering the King and saying to them

'āmḗn 'āmarnā́ l^{e}kṓn
Verily I say unto you

hāy da'ᵃbadtū́n lᵉḥád min 'aḥáy zᵉ'ērayyā́
That which ye did to one of My brethren the least

lī́ 'ᵃbadtūnḗh
to Me ye did it

The parable of the Good Shepherd, John 10¹ ᶠᶠ·, goes straight into rhymed quatrains, with the exception of the second stanza, which on account of its weight stands as a distich.

man dᵉlḗt 'ālḗl bᵉtar'ā́
Whoso that is not entering by the door

lᵉdīrā́ dᵉ'ānā́
into the fold of the sheep,

wᵉsālḗḳ bᵉ'áḥᵃrāyā́
and (is) going up by another (way),

hū́ gannā́b ūlīsṭā'ā́
he (is) a thief and a robber.

hū dᵉ'ītḗh 'ālḗl bᵉtar'ā́
He that is entering by the door,

hū́ rā'ᵃyā́ dᵉ'ānā́
he (is) the shepherd of the sheep.

hādḗn tārā'ā́ pātaḥ lḗh
This one the doorkeeper (is) opening to him,

wᵉ'ānā́ šāmᵉ'ī́n lᵉḳālḗh
and the sheep (are) hearing his voice,

wᵉhū ḳārḗ lᵉdīlḗh bᵉšūmᵉhṓn
and he (is) calling to his own by their name,

ūmappḗḳ lᵉhṓn
and leading out them.

kad 'appḗḳ lᵉdīlḗh kullᵉhṓn
When he has led out his own all of them,

hū́ 'āzḗl ḳōmēhṓn
he (is) going before them,

wᵉ'ānā́ dā́bᵉḳīn léh
and the sheep (are) following him,

d^ehinnū́n makk^erī́n l^eḳālḗh
because they (are) recognizing his voice.

w^enūkrā́ lā dā́b^eḳīn lḗh
And a stranger not they (are) following him,

'ellā́ 'ār^eḳī́n minnḗh
but (are) fleeing from him;

d^elētinnū́n makk^erī́n
because they are not recognizing

ḳāl^ehū́n d^enūḳrī́n
their voice of strangers.

It may be noticed that both examples of rhyme cited from the Fourth Gospel (John $6^{26,27}$, $10^{1ff.}$) are addressed (the first certainly, the second apparently), not to 'the Jews' (i.e. the Rabbinic authorities), but to the *'am hā'āreṣ* or common people, to whom the Synoptic discourses from which we have culled other frequent illustrations of the use of rhyme were directed.

INDEX OF BIBLICAL REFERENCES

PAGE

Genesis
1. 2 . . . 23
4. 23 . . . 48
23, 24 . . . 30, 31, 44, 149
24 . . . 47, 58
27. 29 . . . 149
49. 11 . . . 150

Exodus
15. . . . 24, 60
1 . . . 25, 58
6 . . . 25, 44, 59, 95
9, 10 . . . 60
16 . . . 95

Numbers
12. 3 . . . 167
21. 17 ff. . . . 60
28 . . . 150, 158
23. 3-5 . . . 38
7 . . . 56
7-10 . . . 18
8 . . . 103
24. 21, 22 . . . 150, 151

Deuteronomy
16. 20 . . . 168
32. 1 . . . 60

Judges
5. . . . 24
3 . . . 25
3-5 . . . 33
14. 18 . . . 148
16. 24 . . . 148

1 Samuel
18. 7 . . . 149

2 Samuel
1. 19-27 . . . 24
22 . . . 25, 49
22. . . . 30

Psalms
1. 6 . . . 20
2. 3 . . . 147
5 . . . 147, 148
6 . . . 147
8 . . . 148

PAGE

Psalms (continued)
2. 9 . . . 148
11 . . . 26
3. 2 . . . 21
2-9 . . . 29, 30
3 . . . 58
4 . . . 21
6 . . . 58
7 . . . 47, 58
8 . . . 47, 58
4. 2-9 . . . 25, 26
3 . . . 45
8 . . . 47
9 . . . 49
5. 2-13 . . . 37, 38
4 . . . 55
6 . . . 47, 57
8 . . . 51
12 . . . 47
10. 16 . . . 20
11. 5 . . . 20
15. 1 . . . 105
18. . . . 30
19. 1, 2 . . . 17
2 . . . 102
20. 8 . . . 20, 104
24. 5 . . . 105
7 . . . 45, 54
7-10 . . . 30
9 . . . 45, 54
10 . . . 46
27. 1-6 . . . 36, 37
2 . . . 47
3 . . . 57
4 . . . 50
5 . . . 51, 58
6 . . . 50
29. 1 . . . 95
31. 22 . . . 26
33. 13, 14 . . . 107
40. 1-3 . . . 21
46. 2, 12 . . . 32, 33
6 . . . 57
6, 7 . . . 45
54. 1, 2, 4 . . . 148
92. 9 . . . 95

PAGE

Psalms (continued)
93. 3 95
94. 3 95
9 . . . . . 17, 103
16 17
96. 13 95
101. 7 17
103. 11, 12 108
113. 1 95
114. 1–8 . . . . . 16, 17
118. 26 146
121. . . . . . 95, 96
127. 1 108

Proverbs
1. 11, 15, 16 159
15, 16 157
2. 2, 3 . . . . . 158, 159
6, 7 157
17 159
3. 5, 6 158
7, 8 157
13, 14 . . . . . 157, 158
21, 22 157
23, 24 158
4. 8, 9 158
12, 13 158
20, 21 157
24, 25 158
5. 3, 4 . . . . . 157, 158
7–14 . . . 154–156, 158
9, 10 158
17, 18 158
6. 16–19 22
7. 2, 3 157
8, 9 . . . . . 158, 159
8. 1 159
9. 1 159
13 159
10. 1, 7 20
7 104
12. 5 104
13. 24, 25 . . . . . 158, 159
15. 19 21
21. 12 159
22. 18, 19 157
23. 1, 2 158
31. 10 159
26 159

Ecclesiasticus
4. 22, 23 157
29, 30 157
6. 3 159
25–27 157
7. 18 159
21 159

PAGE

Ecclesiasticus (continued)
9. 1, 2 157
3 158
6, 7 157
15, 16 157
11. 7, 8, 9 159
8, 9 158
12. 12 157
13. 4–7 156
15, 16 157
14. 1, 2 157
23, 24 157
15. 2, 3 158
7, 8 158
16. 7, 8, 9, 10 158
11, 12 157
24, 25 157
30. 23 158
31. 4 157
35. 24, 25 157
36. 18, 19 157
20, 21 157
29 159
38. 16–23 . . . . 51, 52, 53
16 . . . . . 156, 158
17, 18, 23 156
41. 9 158
43. 28, 29 158
44. 1–8 159
45. 4 167
19 158
46. 9 158
19 157

Song of Songs
5. 1 153
6. 1–3 152
8. 1–3 . . . . . 151, 152
6 . . . . . 152, 153

Isaiah
1. 4 . . . . . 44, 55
4–6 . . . . . 28, 29
5, 6 45
6 57
10–17 . . . . . 40, 41
12 58
13 45
14 48
15 58
16 54
21 54
21–23 40
23 46
14. 8 39
33. 2 . . . . . 48, 51

PAGE

Isaiah (continued)
33. 2–5 . . . . . 26, 27
3 48
4 . . . . . 45, 46
13 . . . . . 48, 58
13–16 27
14 . . . . . 51, 55
15 . . . . . 49, 53
16 54
16, 17 51
40. 29–31 19
51. 7 . . . . 48, 54, 55
7–8 31
8 . . . . 46, 49, 58
17–20 42
55. 1 ff. 168
6, 7 19
61. 1 167

Jeremiah
48. 17 40

Lamentations
1. 1 40
2. 1 40
19 42
3. 1–9 35
6 . . . . . . 49, 54
8 58
9 50
12 39
14, 15, 18, 23 50
35, 48, 66 56
4. 1 40

Habakkuk
2. 1 38
3. 60
3. 17 61

Daniel
2. 4–7. 28 109
4. 3 109
11, 12 109
12 111
14 . . . . . . 110, 111
17 110
22 111
27 110
29 111
30 111
5. 10 111
17 111
20, 21 . . . . 111, 112

Amos
5. 2 . . . 33, 44, 46, 50, 57
21–24 . . . . . 18, 19
24 105

PAGE

Micah
6. 6 . . . . . . 49, 53
6–8 31
7 . . . . . . 46, 56
8 58

Matthew
5. 3 ff. 130
3–11 . . . . 165, 166
6 92
9–13 . . . . 112, 113
14–16 . . . 130, 131, 171
14, 15 . . . . 72, 77, 107
17 92
19 77
19–21 115
19, 20 . . . 76, 87, 88, 115
22, 23 . . . 76, 99, 131, 171
23 92
24 . . . . 99, 116, 123
25 67
34 92
39, 40 . . . . 114, 169
44 . . . . . . 67, 114
45 . . . . . . 67, 87
48 114
7. 1, 2. 114
3–5 82
6 . . . 68, 69, 103, 131, 132, 169
7, 8 . . . . 67, 114, 115
11 82
13, 14 . . . 76, 87, 88, 137
14 106
15 77
17 . . . . . 72, 76, 104
22, 23 137
8. 12 68
20 . . . . 106, 132, 169
9. 15–17 . . . . . 88, 140
16 141
10. 5–7 . . . . . 121, 122
8–16 . . . . . 121, 123
17–22 . . 88, 119, 120, 121, 122, 123
23 . . . . . . 120, 122
24, 25 . . . . . 67, 87
24–27 . . . . 121, 122, 123
25 83
26 65
28 92
32, 33 76
34 92
39 . . . . . . 73, 77
40 91
41 69

PAGE

Matthew (continued)

11. 4–6 . . . 117
12 . . . 68, 87
23 . . . 77
25–29 . . . 133
25–27 . . . 77, 133, 171
28–30 . . . 144, 145
12. 8 . . . 98
11, 12, 25 . . . 64
30 . . . 68, 132
31, 32 . . . 65
32 . . . 74
33 . . . 76, 99
35 . . . 77, 79
39 . . . 92
13. 12 . . . 74
16, 17 . . . 145
31 ff. . . . 65
42 . . . 68
50 . . . 68
52 . . . 116, 123
15. 1–20 . . . 74
11 . . . 72, 74
14 . . . 133, 170
16. 4 . . . 92
9 . . . 66
17–19 . . . 117, 123
19 . . . 78
24 . . . 66
24–27 . . . 141, 142
25 . . . 74, 85
17. 17 . . . 66, 87
18. 5 . . . 91
15 . . . 79
18 . . . 78
21, 22 . . . 79
19. 6 . . . 75
14 . . . 66
17 . . . 106
26 . . . 75, 85, 87
30 . . . 75
20. 16 . . . 73, 75
22 ff. . . . 63, 64
22. 13 . . . 68
14 . . . 78
23. 5–10 . . . 89
12 . . . 73, 77, 104
27, 28 . . . 78
29 . . . 68, 87, 103
37–39 . . . 146
24. 7 . . . 66
9–14 . . . 119, 120
29 . . . 66, 87
35 . . . 75
50, 51 . . . 68
25. 1 ff. . . . 116
25. 21, 23 . . . 78
30 . . . 68
31 ff. . . . 172–174, 142–143
26. 11 . . . 76, 85
41 . . . 75

Mark

2. 19–22 . . . 88, 140, 141
27 . . . 73, 98
3. 4 . . . 64
24, 25 . . . 64
28, 29 . . . 65, 74
4. 22 . . . 65
24 . . . 114
25 . . . 74
30 . . . 65
6. 7 . . . 121
8–11 . . . 121
7. 8 . . . 104
8, 9 . . . 74
15 . . . 74
34–38 . . . 141, 142
8. 12 . . . 92
17, 18 . . . 65, 66
34 . . . 66
35 . . . 74, 85
9. 19 . . . 66, 87
37 . . . 91
43 . . . 106
45 . . . 106
10. 9 . . . 75
14 . . . 66
27 . . . 75, 85
31 . . . 75
38 ff. . . . 63, 64
13. 8 . . . 66, 118, 120
9–13 . . . 88, 118, 119, 120
14 . . . 120
24–27 . . . 118
24, 25 . . . 66, 87
25 . . . 106
31 . . . 75
14. 7 . . . 38, 75, 76, 85, 86

Luke

4. 18 . . . 167
5. 3–11 . . . 165, 166
20 . . . 123, 167
34–39 . . . 88, 140
6. 5 . . . 98
9 . . . 64
9–13 . . . 161
20 . . . 123, 167
27–29 . . . 67, 113, 114, 123, 169
35 . . . 67, 87

	PAGE
Luke (continued)	
6. 36–38	114, 123
39	133, 170
41, 42	82
43	76, 99
45	77, 99
7. 22, 23	117, 124
8. 17	65
9. 1	121
3–5	121
23	66
23–26	141, 142
24	74, 85
26	142
41	66, 87
48	91
58	132, 169
62	132, 170
10. 3	121
5	121
6	121
12	121
15	77
16	91, 124
21, 22	77, 133, 171
23, 24	145
41, 42	145
11. 1	123
2–4	113
9, 10	67, 114, 115, 123
13	82
17	64
23	68, 132
29	92
34	76, 92, 99, 131
34, 35, 36	131
47	68, 87
12. 5	92
8	76
11, 12	119
22, 23	67
32–37	115, 123
33	76, 87, 88, 115
33, 34	115, 170, 171
35, 36	116
42, 43	116, 123
46	68
47, 48	78
48	69, 107
49–51	90
51	92
13. 8	66
18	65
23–27	137
24	76, 87, 88
28	68

	PAGE
Luke (continued)	
14. 11	77
16–24	78
15. 32	69
16. 10	78, 105
11, 12	83
13	99, 116
15	78
16	68, 87
25	78
17. 3	79
33	77, 85
18. 14	77
16	66
27	75, 85, 87
19. 43, 44	69
21. 10	66
12	120
12–17	88
12–19	119
25, 26	66, 87
33	75
22. 25, 26	64
23. 28	79
31	83
24. 38	70
John	
3. 6	72, 79, 105
11	70, 97, 103, 133
12	83
14	97
18	72, 79, 97, 129
19	97
20, 21	79, 107, 129
31	79
34	97
35	130
36	79, 106
37	130
4. 13, 14	79
22	79, 98
36	70, 98, 106, 134, 136
5. 24	106
29	80, 106
40	106
43	80
47	83
6. 26	106
26, 27	136, 170, 175
27	80, 106
32	80, 98
33	106
35	70, 103, 130, 134
37	93, 130

	PAGE
John (continued)	
53	106
55	70, 134
63	106, 134, 136
7. 6	80
34	70
37	70
8. 12	134, 135
23	80
31, 32	135
32	93
34	70
34–36	135, 136
35	72, 80, 136
37	70
39	135, 136
44	90
9. 39	73, 80
41	80
10. 1–5	136, 174, 175
10	80, 106
11	93
26, 27	94
11. 9	107
9, 10	81
25	93
12. 8	76, 81, 85
12. 24, 25	81
26	70
31	71
13. 16	71, 103, 136
20	91
14. 1–10	126 ff.
2, 3	93
15	129
18	129
19	81
21	93, 129
23, 24	129
27	71, 129
15. 2	81
5	129
13, 14	93
15	81
26	71
16. 7	94
20–22	144
20	94
22	94
33	81
18. 36	94
20. 17	71
27	71, 104

www.ingramcontent.com/pod-product-compliance
Lightning Source LLC
Chambersburg PA
CBHW050807160426
43192CB00010B/1669
* 9 7 8 1 6 0 6 0 8 2 9 5 9 *